D0407801

More Praise for *The Human Brand*

"Today's technology makes it appear as if marketing has become more complex. In fact, it hasn't — especially for those brands who think and act like 'the shop on the corner.' People's connection to what they buy and whom they buy it from is what's important. That's been the same for generations. The challenge is in making large brands appear 'small.' *The Human Brand* cuts through the complexities of 'marketing local' in the digital age to tell the simple truth: connections are key."

—**Patrick Doyle**, president and chief executive officer,
Domino's Pizza, Inc.

"How do we earn the lasting loyalty of others? Chris and Susan provide fundamental, yet powerful, insights into building relationships that matter. They challenge us to 'come out from behind the curtain' and lead with courage, conviction, and heart. Never before has the humanization of brands and leadership been so vital to success."

—**Jay Gould**, president and chief executive officer,
American Standard Brands

"By re-focusing us on the primal foundations of survival, *The Human Brand* takes a major, comprehensive step towards understanding the real drivers of commercial success. If you care about what ignites, engages, and sustains deep, strong relationships with your brand and company, read this book."

—**Susan Fournier**, coauthor, *Consumer-Brand Relationships*,
and professor, Boston University School of Management

"In all the noise and all the confusion, the insights on what really matters for corporations to maintain true customer loyalty make *The Human Brand* invaluable."

—**John Williams**, president and chief executive officer, Domtar
Corporation

"The insights detailed in *The Human Brand* have completely reshaped our thinking and approach to building lasting alumni relationships and financial support. Our resurgent alumni results in both areas are a testament to the timely and timeless value of warmth, competence, and worthy intentions."

—**Daniel J. Curran**, president, University of Dayton

"Malone and Fiske offer compelling new evidence on the dangers of excess focus on short-term shareholder value. Their anecdote-rich book is helpful for any business concerned with how to retain customer loyalty and trust in these complex times."

—**Noreena Hertz**, author, *The Silent Takeover* and *Eyes Wide Open*, and professor, Duisenberg School of Finance

"The important insights in *The Human Brand* help explain why B Corporations are able to attract the best talent and the most evangelical customers, and why they deliver lasting benefits to our society and to shareholders."

—**Jay Coen Gilbert**, cofounder, B Lab

CHRIS MALONE | SUSAN T. FISKE

THE
HUMAN
BRAND

How We Relate to

PEOPLE, PRODUCTS, AND COMPANIES

JB JOSSEY-BASS™
A Wiley Brand

Cover design by: Adrian Morgan
Cover image : © Robert Churchill | Getty Images

Published by Jossey-Bass
A Wiley Brand

One Montgomery Street, Suite 1200, San Francisco, CA 94104-4594—www.josseybass.com

Jossey-Bass books and products are available through most bookstores. To contact Jossey-
Bass directly call our Customer Care Department within the U.S. at 800-956-7739,
outside the U.S. at 317-572-3986, or fax 317-572-4002.

Wiley publishes in a variety of print and electronic formats and by print-on-demand.
Some material included with standard print versions of this book may not be included
in e-books or in print-on-demand. If this book refers to media such as a CD or DVD that
is not included in the version you purchased, you may download this material at http://
booksupport.wiley.com. For more information about Wiley products, visit www.wiley.com.

Library of Congress Cataloging-in-Publication Data

Malone, Chris, 1969-
     The human brand : how we relate to people, products, and companies / Chris
Malone, Susan T. Fiske. — First edition.
        1 online resource.
     Includes index.
     Description based on print version record and CIP data provided by publisher;
resource not viewed.
        ISBN 978-1-118-75815-1 (pdf) — ISBN 978-1-118-75827-4 (epub) —
     ISBN 978-1-118-61131-9 (hardback)
        1. Consumer behavior. 2. Marketing—Psychological aspects.   I. Fiske,
Susan T. II. Title.
     HF5415.32
     658.8'342—dc23   2013028032

Printed in the United States of America
FIRST EDITION
HB Printing 10 9 8 7 6 5 4 3 2 1

For my beautiful wife, Beth, and our remarkable sons, Charlie, Henry, and Patrick. You will always be my greatest love, passion, pride, and inspiration. CM

For my inspiring husband, Doug Massey, and our wonderful children, Geoff, Lydia, and Vanessa. Our twenty-first-century family is my cherished delight in every way. STF

Contents

Acknowledgments   xi

Introduction: Back to the Future   1
Why our immediate future so strongly resembles our distant past

1   Warmth and Competence   19
The two timeless judgments that drive our behavior toward others

2   The Loyalty Test   39
Why we expect companies and brands to commit to us first

3   The Principle of Worthy Intentions   61
The simple and reliable way to demonstrate warmth and competence

4   The Price of Progress   85
How faceless commerce leads to a focus on discounts

5   Take Us to Your Leader   105
What we learn from the people behind the things we buy

6   Show Your True Colors   127
Why mistakes and crises are a golden loyalty opportunity

7   The Relationship Renaissance   151
Navigating the road ahead

Notes   169
About the Authors   185
Index   187

THE
HUMAN
BRAND

Acknowledgments

We hope the readers of this book will find it useful, both as customers and as people who think about customers.

No book is an island, and we are grateful to the community of contributors that helped produce it. First, we thank our agent, Jim Levine, who saw its promise, and Jill Totenberg, who supported our early vision. Our editor, Karen Murphy, has guided us from proposal to final form, and we are grateful. Noel Weyrich and Bruce Tucker ably helped us develop the shape and voice of the text, as well as encouraged us to hone and focus our ideas. We thank them each for their thoughtful and constructive guidance.

Much of the most relevant academic research on the warmth and competence model comes from Nicolas Kervyn, who was a postdoctoral visitor and collaborator, and from other members of Susan's Fiske Lab at Princeton. Research on its implications for companies and brands was assisted by Chris's colleagues at Fidelum Partners, including Candice Bennett, Bill Bule, Rick Carpenter, Donald Crawford, Leanne Fesenmeyer, Kennan Kosenko, Steve McMahon, Ashley Phillips, Michael Sinclair, and Erica Seidel.

And we would especially like to thank the experts from various companies and brands, who gave generously of their time for interviews with Chris. These included John Beadle, Greg Brown, Steve Cannon, Tim Cost, Bob Dekoy, Mike Faherty, Kelly Faddis, Joe Hage, Dave Harper, Linda Jenkinson, Peter Kaye, Grace Kim,

Michael Kolleth, Sundar Kumarasamy, Tom Laforge, Ed Martin, Pedro Massa, Andrew Parkinson, Andrew Rondepierre, Fred Rost, Stan Sthanunathan, and Russell Weiner.

In addition, we received valuable input, suggestions, and contributions from many enthusiastic supporters, including Jill Avery, Angela Cason, Barry Gesserman, Ilan Geva, Peter Glick, Noreena Hertz, Ken Kozielski, Michael Lowenstein, Victoria Porter, Sean Otto, Gary Schanzer, and Frank Strunk, for which we are extremely grateful. In particular, Ed Wallace, with his work on business relationships, was the catalyst that inspired Chris to pursue the path that led him to Susan, and ultimately to this book. We offer our sincere thanks to each of you.

Finally, we are grateful to our respective families, who encouraged us and tolerated the disruption while we met our accelerated production schedule. They are competent and warm beyond belief, and we are sustained by their continued love and support.

Introduction:
Back to the Future

Why our immediate future so strongly resembles our distant past

In late May 2000, the reality television game show *Survivor* debuted in the homes of fifteen million American viewers. The show offered a glimpse into our tribal past with a modern twist—a $1 million prize for the winning contestant. It was launched soon after Memorial Day, at the start of the summer ratings doldrums. However, by the time *Survivor* reached its first-season finale in late August, its following had grown to more than fifty-one million viewers, second in ratings that year only to the Super Bowl.[1]

Over the subsequent dozen years or so, *Survivor* has proven to be one of the most durable ratings franchises for the CBS broadcast network. It has spawned an entire industry of "last player standing" reality show knockoffs. What accounts for such extreme popularity? Perhaps it's how all these shows tap into something we are hard-wired to recognize and appreciate—the primeval human struggle for survival and the remarkable skills we

1

all possess to perceive, judge, and form mutually supportive relationships in order to survive. *Survivor* and all its imitators offer us insights into the eternal, into the essence of being human, rooted in our prehistoric past.

Social psychologists have deduced that primitive humans were forced, in their struggle for existence, to develop a primal, unconscious ability to make two specific kinds of judgments with a high degree of speed and sufficient accuracy: What are the intentions of other people toward me? How capable are they of carrying out those intentions? Today we judge others almost instantly along these same two categories of social perception, which are known as *warmth* and *competence*.

A person who demonstrates both warmth and competence inspires feelings of trust and admiration within us, motivating us to seek a continuing relationship with that person. One who displays competence in the absence of warmth, however, tends to leave us feeling envious and suspicious, while someone we perceive as warm but not competent stimulates feelings of pity and sympathy. A person who exhibits low levels of both warmth *and* competence often provokes feelings of contempt and disgust.

Survival for our distant ancestors depended upon their ability to quickly judge others according to these criteria. Humans have come to dominate the globe using this deeply programmed social circuitry, painstakingly developed and tested for ages through the harsh, unforgiving process of natural selection. This, the original real-life game of *Survivor*, still shapes all our social interactions today.

We are merely the latest in a line of thousands of generations to inherit this time-tested ability, and we apply it in *all* our relationships, including those involving commercial transactions. We engage with brands and the companies behind them on same basis of warmth and competence because, no different from people, companies and brands have the capacity to stir up these hard-wired primal passions. We experience feelings of affection and admiration for brands and companies that do well by us, and we feel insult or even rage when we believe that those companies have treated us badly.

An Email to Princeton

Chris first stumbled upon academic research on warmth and competence in 2009 and wondered if the social science behind its insights might help explain the kinds of loyalty and relationships we form with companies and brands. Having previously marketed products at both Procter & Gamble and Coca-Cola, as well as promoted professional athletes at the NBA and NHL, he wrote a white paper that integrated warmth and competence theory with customer relationship research. In May, 2010, Chris sent a copy of the white paper in an unsolicited email to Susan with the heading "I've become a fan of your work . . ." He proposed meeting for lunch to discuss possible areas of research collaboration.

As Princeton's Eugene Higgins Professor, of Psychology and Public Affairs, Susan has researched and written extensively about how perceptions of warmth and competence contribute to the common human tendencies toward stereotyping, prejudice, and discrimination. For twenty years or more, she has documented how popular perceptions of ethnic, gender, and occupational group members held by the society at large lead to stereotyped images, emotional prejudices, and discriminatory behavior toward individuals within those groups.

From her childhood, Susan had experienced the contrasting values of warmth and competence as embodied by her two grandmothers. Her father's mother was a warm and kind woman, a classic grandma. Susan's earliest memories recall her grandmother reaching into her huge purse to retrieve candy and Golden books to read aloud on long car rides. Susan's grandmother on the other side of her family was very different. She was a distant but admirable figure, a Harvard-trained economist who, according to family legend, conducted the first unemployment census in Massachusetts. But Susan does not remember her as a warm and comfy grandmother.

Years later, as Susan pondered how to balance family and career, and the seeming need to trade off between warmth and competence, as her grandmothers had done, she grew more curious about the subject and began to conduct experiments and surveys to explore it in depth. As Susan developed the theory of warmth and competence, her studies and those of other researchers showed that as much as 82 percent of our judgments of others can be predicted by these two categories of perception.[2]

Not long after Chris and Susan's first conversation, the two began researching the application of warmth and competence theory to companies and brands. Beginning in June 2010, this unique collaboration has evaluated more than forty-five companies and brands in ten separate studies. The research documents the extent to which many major companies and brands are perceived as lacking in both warmth and competence. They are seen as selfish, greedy, and concerned only with their own immediate gain. In fact, nearly every one of the companies and brands studied in this research has fallen short of customer expectations for honesty and worthy intentions—behaviors indicative of warmth and competence.

The research also reveals striking psychological evidence for why people hate banks, oil companies, and cable companies so much. The constant pressure for faster and larger profits has steered companies in these and other industries into violating all the prerequisites for trust that we all unconsciously expect of them. And yet, there is another side to this coin. When companies held in high esteem for warmth and competence make errors and stumble, they are able to recover from those errors, building even more genuine, trusting, and lasting relationships with customers. We prefer to forgive companies we like, as we would other people we like, if we value the relationships and perceive that their intentions were good.

These insights arrive at a time of rapid change and uncertainty in our economic life. Large companies and brands that once seemed invincible are struggling and steadily losing market share, calling into question much of what they believed about running a successful business. American Airlines is besieged by smaller, friendlier Southwest just as Gap has been besieged by Lululemon. And who can forget Blockbuster, the once-dominant video rentals service, noteworthy for profiting on its punitive late-return fees. The company was bankrupted within a span of a few years when Netflix came along with a penalty-free DVD rental system that represented a healthier relationship between company profit and customer satisfaction.

Americans have decided that bigger is no longer better, and in the case of some of America's best-known brands, bigger may be much worse. At the same time, lots of smaller companies and brands are growing rapidly and filling the void with far fewer resources and a very different approach to doing business. Many of these upstarts are guided by purpose-driven missions that say as much about who they are as people as it does about the products and services they provide. They speak to us more intimately, and they appeal to our natural need for warmth and competence.

The growing divide between big national brands and their customers has been decades in the making. In the eyes of customers, old-line companies don't listen; they advertise. They don't adjust themselves to our needs; they try to sell us what they've got. They aren't flexible, because they have strict policies to ensure consistency and efficiency—and deadening, impersonal aloofness. For as long as anyone reading this book has been alive, big companies and the people who work in them have been in the habit of shaping our expectations in the exact opposite direction of our natural desires for warmth and competence.

The Middle Ages of Marketing

In 1882, the French painter Édouard Manet unveiled his impressionist masterpiece, *A Bar at the Folies-Bergère*. The painting depicts a simple scene with a young barmaid at its center, posing behind a counter lined with libations. In the far right-hand corner of the canvas, a brown bottle of ale is shown with a distinctive bright red triangle on its label—the unmistakable trademark of British brewer Bass & Co. *A Bar at the Folies-Bergère* would be Manet's last major work before his death in 1883 at age fifty-one, but the painting bears one other curious distinction. It is perhaps the first-ever depiction of a commercial trademark in a work of fine art.

Like most cities in Europe and the United States, Paris in 1882 was undergoing rapid transformation. The Industrial Revolution was in full bloom. Daily life was changing fast and forever, as traditional agrarian societies on both sides of the Atlantic embraced modernity, and urban populations exploded due to the ever-rising demand for factory workers. In the U.S. economy, the rapid expansion of national railway networks and telegraph lines prompted the evolution of mass production, packaging, retailing, and advertising. The first national product brands arrived on the scene, including some that survive to this day, such as Levi Strauss, Tabasco, and Heinz. It was in the 1880s that, in the words of one historian, masses of people became dependent for the first time ever on "goods made by unknown hands."[3]

The people who produced those goods faced a number of obstacles in profitably selling them. It may be hard to believe today, but humans were never mentally wired to trust and enjoy goods made by "unknown hands." Before the advent of mass production, mass distribution, and mass media, people in every culture in all of world history knew their butchers, bakers, and candlestick makers by name. Before 1880, there were hardly any packaged goods or ready-to-wear clothing. There were no fixed prices for goods, and often barter was substituted for money.[4] For all these reasons, commercial exchange entailed little distinction between the seller and the product or service offered. Customers were, in effect, buying the person who stood behind the product along with the product itself. And human transactions of all kinds had been that way for so long that we have within us an embedded preference for trusting, face-to-face exchanges in all our affairs.

This was the challenge faced by the people responsible for the earliest brands: brand symbols like the Bass Ale triangle or the Heinz label keystone were impersonal and abstract, while humans prefer the personal and concrete. Military leaders, for instance, have always known that abstract ideas, such as patriotism and freedom, are not enough to inspire and motivate soldiers to risk their lives in battle. Military training all around the world is designed to nurture what already is the natural inclination of men fighting in groups—to fight for their buddies, to fight for each other, to protect and care for the group.[5] In a similar way, people in the 1880s were well practiced in being loyal to the local tailor or shoemaker, whom they regarded as a friend. Now, with a national economy reliant on strangers selling to other strangers, how could people be persuaded, against human nature, to be loyal to an abstract brand instead?

In *New and Improved: The Story of Mass Marketing in America*, Richard Tedlow explains how the Montgomery Ward company tried to humanize its mail-order catalogue by publishing pictures of the company's founders, executives, and even the heads of individual product lines. Beneath those pictures, their signatures appeared as guarantees of customer satisfaction. These little touches had their desired effect, as evidenced by the following excerpt of a letter from a customer found in Montgomery Ward's archives:

> I suppose you wonder why we haven't ordered anything
> from you since the fall. Well, the cow kicked my arm

and broke it and besides my wife was sick, and there was the doctor bill. But now, thank God, that is paid, and we are all well again, and we have a fat new baby boy, and please send plush bonnet number 29d8077 . . .

Here was a man unselfconsciously responding to Montgomery Ward's mass marketing message as though he had a personal relationship with the catalogue's employees. Tedlow wrote, "The letter strikes one as mildly ludicrous, but also rather touching in both tone and content, because the author was transferring a community attitude that would be quite appropriate when dealing with a local country storekeeper to the context of a mass-selling situation in which the merchant neither knew the producer nor cared about him or her as an individual."[6]

Modern marketing and advertising also grew up in response to this challenge of goods made by unknown hands. Prior to 1880, advertising was a tiny business, almost entirely limited to small-type notices squeezed in between the stories in newspapers. By 1900, advertising had blossomed into a huge $600-million industry that accounted for 4 percent of the national income, a percentage that remained unchanged for the following sixty years.[7]

Advertising was able to communicate the positive qualities of mass manufactured goods in ways that personalized them. Aside from low prices and wide variety, industrial processes also guaranteed a high degree of product consistency, something hard to come by in preindustrial society. And reliability actually does appeal to our cognitively miserly minds, which generally resist surprises (unless, as Susan has written before, the surprise comes with party hats).[8]

Take the example of Procter & Gamble's Ivory soap, one of the first mass-marketed products, with a brand name and selling proposition that clearly appealed to our penchant for predictability and easily categorized experiences. Many of us have fond, familiar associations with Ivory soap, which make it seem like an old family friend. The Ivory name was selected for its associa-tion with wholesomeness and cleanliness. Its buoyancy gave the customer further assurance that it was, as claimed, 99.44 percent pure. Ivory's chief features and benefits were: "As good as the fin-est Castile soaps, but significantly cheaper." By the end of the nineteenth century, the basic elements of modern branding were in place, epitomized by products such as Ivory soap.

This decisive move away from merely identifying a product by its maker's name and toward public images and symbolic branding led companies to a singular insight: the secret to commercial suc-cess lay in creating a brand with its own image, reputation, and emotional appeal. This was a powerful insight at the time, but in later years, it would prove to be a *blinding* insight: Ever since then, brand owners haven't been able to see past it. The huge leaps in scale, efficiency, and profitability generated during the Industrial Revolution led businesses and their academic counterparts to the regrettable conclusion that interactions with customers could be standardized and automated in a similar fashion with enhanced effect.

The introduction of radio and television—momentous inno-vations in human communication—only helped reinforce the limited one-way relationships brands maintained with consum-ers. Mass-media messages were necessarily tailored to a "one-size-fits-all" format. Today we get a crushing load of this information, as many as five thousand messages per day, up from a mere five hundred commercial messages per day in the 1970s.[9]

It is a commonly held myth that mass communication her-alded a kind of golden age of brand marketing and customer loy-alty. In truth, mass communication has systematically eliminated meaningful customer relationships and diluted brand loyalty. The sexy "golden age" of advertising portrayed in the wildly popular series *Mad Men* fostered the illusion that creativity, aspirational images, and big advertising budgets were all that brands needed to achieve and sustain success. As a result, customers who were once known by name were transformed into nameless, faceless "consumers," broken into demographic sectors to be conquered in the quest for market share.

In his 1994 book *The Naked Consumer*, Erik Larson noted how a 1991 letter from a publishing house declined his request to be removed from its mailing list. "We regret that this request cannot be accommodated, as we rent all of our mailing lists and therefore exercise no control over their content . . . I would like to be more helpful, but my hands are tied." The publishing house president cared enough to write, but only to inform Larson that he didn't care enough to have his company manage its own mailing lists. Larson complained of how marketers had built "a vast intelligence network" of demographic information providers, "all for the lofty goal of finding more irresistible ways to sell us more soaps, laxatives and detergents."[10]

By artificially separating the producers of products and services from their end customers, the industrial revolution introduced middle players such as distributors and retailers to mediate relationships between producer and customer. Producers came to believe that the mass communication of features, benefits, and positioning would be enough to yield lasting customer loyalty, without actually having to deal directly with or even know the names of those individual customers.

These and other myths, from what we call the Middle Ages of Marketing, are now being shattered every day. Customers are now abandoning many of the largest and most established consumer brands in favor of smaller companies with fewer resources and very different ways of doing business. We are increasingly calling it quits on the long but often shallow relationships we've had with many of the world's largest and most established companies and brands—all because newer, more transparent and trustworthy ones have come along that appreciate us more and treat us better.

The Relationship Renaissance

The following chapters will explore the many dimensions of warmth and competence in order to shed new light on why companies like Domino's, Lululemon, Zappos, and Chobani have surged in popularity while other tradition-bound brands have been flagging. Whether intentionally or not, their philosophy and practices demonstrate the worthy intentions we unconsciously expect.

Our research also documents how the big banks, oil companies, and airlines have all developed policies and practices that are fundamentally at odds with the spontaneous triggers of human warmth and competence. The Internet, social networks, and mobile communications all have worked together to undermine previously powerful forces in the economy. We contend that a new Relationship Renaissance between customer and company is emerging out of the Middle Ages of Marketing. Customers already have near-instantaneous power to pass judgment on how companies and brands conduct themselves in public. That power will continue to grow for decades to come.

Chapter One explores the extent to which our warmth and competence judgments drive our interactions with all kinds of social groups, including companies and brands. Our study of the most passionately loyal Coca-Cola customers, for instance, revealed that perceptions of Coke's warmth and competence were almost twice as persuasive in purchasing decisions as the features and benefits of the beverage alone.

Chapter Two discusses why the short-term-profit focus of most companies almost guarantees that they will tend to seek exploitive relationships with even their most loyal customers. We introduce the Loyalty Test as a way of gauging the quality of any relationship in terms of warmth and competence.

Chapter Three looks at the other side of the story: the companies who have earned our fanatical loyalty *because* they succeed in connecting with our need for warmth and competence. Companies that put the customers' interests ahead of their own, in accord with the principle of *worthy intentions*, are able to prosper financially by activating our automatic perceptions of their warmth and competence.

Chapter Four entertains the idea that while mobile and internet technologies have energized the Relationship Renaissance, they can also serve to eliminate warmth and humanity from our economic exchanges. We contrast the practices of Amazon, which has reduced prices by using automation to minimize human interaction with customers, with those of Zappos, which uses technology to enable its "customer-obsessed" culture.

Chapter Five explains how highly visible and outspoken business leaders inspire loyalty in their companies and brands because each puts a human face on their respective company's intentions and capabilities. Many large companies insulate their leaders from public view and rely instead on logos, advertising, and technology to communicate with customers. We show how companies that ignore our basic need to relate to human faces are likely to lose in the marketplace during the Relationship Renaissance.

In Chapter Six, we discuss our research that shows setbacks and problems can provide companies with opportunities to build stronger relationships with customers—as long as these troubles are handled with worthy intentions. Product recalls and other embarrassments are seen by customers as rare moments of truth in which companies and brands are able to demonstrate whether they care more about the best interests of their customers or their own profits.

The final chapter offers some specific guidance for navigating the Relationship Renaissance that lies ahead. To achieve sustained success, companies and brands will need to become more self-aware and mindful of their customers' warmth and competence perceptions, as well as more willing to adapt the way they do business in response to them. It won't be easy, especially for publicly traded companies, but there is hope on the horizon for organizations of all kinds to achieve more balanced and sustained prosperity for all of their stakeholders.

Instant Karma

The next time you hear the expression "baker's dozen," try to picture a worried bread maker in medieval England, bagging up a dozen rolls and then throwing in an extra one—just as insurance against getting fined or pilloried in the town square. For centuries, the sales of bread and beer, staples of English life, were ruled by strict common-law provisions on commercial weights and measures. A dozen rolls of bread could not be sold below a certain weight, or the social consequences for the baker might be grave. To be on the safe side, bakers habitually added a bonus roll or two, which came to be known as "in-bread."[11]

Old-time methods of social humiliation such as the pillory were abolished by the middle of the nineteenth century, but small-town and neighborhood merchants always had to be careful to protect their reputations. Their trust-based relationships with the people they knew were what kept customers coming back. If a small business or local merchant wronged someone, everyone in town would know about it by the end of weekend worship. Those who failed to make it right might be put out of business or run out of town.

Rituals of ostracism, shunning, and public shaming are found in most tribal cultures going back to the recesses of history. Our need for belonging is so deep that the fear of becoming an outcast has provided enough social pressure to keep most people honest.[12] Merchants accepted that the relationships they had with their customers were critical to their survival, and they either learned to nurture those relationships or faced financial ruin.

This relational orientation survives today in pockets: the coffee shop owner who knows your favorite type of joe-to-go and remakes it if your triple-shot is shorted. Ditto the corner storekeeper who trusts you to pay later when you've left your wallet at home. The local dry cleaner might stay open just a few minutes later for you if you call ahead. And you, in turn, reward these gestures of benevolence with your loyalty and word-of-mouth recommendations. But if your local merchants should fail these little tests, your neighbors will hear about that, too. Pillories are long gone, but the modern, verbal equivalent of rotten tomatoes endures.

For most of the modern era, however, national brands and their parent companies have been all but exempt from such forms of public censure. In practical terms, there has been almost nothing we could do as customers to expose or punish brands we found unworthy of the public's trust. We had no avenues to impress upon them the importance of what most small businesspeople and local tradespeople have always had to live with—social accountability.

Until now. Social accountability—that most natural and essential check on human behavior—has reentered our national commercial culture for the first time in 150 years, care of the Internet. It's not overstating the case to assert that for the first time in history, the entire world is wired in a way that is consistent with the way evolution has wired us to think and behave. We judge brands, companies, and institutions the way we have always judged people for millennia—fast, categorically, and on a very individual basis. For the first time, everyone has the potential to share those judgments with millions of other like-minded individuals.

We truly live in a global village, one in which social networks, bloggers, online reviews, and crowds of protesters can be roused at the drop of a hashtag. The one-time small-community concern that "everybody in town might know by weekend worship" has evolved into "everybody on earth might know by tomorrow morning." Social networks have ensured that the threat of "instant karma"—the norm in all commercial exchanges prior to the Industrial Revolution—is now feared by even the world's largest corporations. Social media aren't so much changing the rules of business as they are restoring those rules to their natural order of social accountability. They make it clear that long-lived business-as-usual practices will have to change or die.

The interplay of broadband internet, social media, and mobile communications is what University of Toronto professor Barry Wellman has dubbed a "triple revolution" in human interaction. It could be that this triple revolution has reached a watershed moment in the power of social accountability. Wellman notes that the old adage about the power of the print media ("Never pick a fight with someone who buys ink by the barrel") needs to be updated as follows: "Never pick a fight with someone who is networked with strong internet and mobile connections."[13]

Consider the instant karma that came to Verizon one day in December 2011. Verizon announced a new $2 convenience fee for online bill payments—on a Thursday afternoon during the dead week between Christmas and New Year's. If Verizon managers were hoping no one was paying attention, they were wrong. Twitter, Facebook, and the rest of the Web all lit up instantly with howls of protest, online petitions, and denunciations of the company. The backlash forced Verizon to drop the fee the next day, less than twenty-four hours after plans for it were announced.[14] Instant karma, indeed.

Social accountability of this kind is here to stay, because customers now have the power to influence outcomes that once were far beyond their control. But there are two sides to instant karma. Social networks not only empower customers but also provide the direct access to customers that brands and companies require in order to reestablish, develop, and sustain meaningful relationships with their customers.

With the waning of the Middle Ages of Marketing (the age of mass everything), the Relationship Renaissance constitutes a rebirth of preindustrial values, of an age in which customers can again insist on personal relationships with their product and service providers. For all businesses, large or small, a consistent focus on building personal relationships with customers will be an essential ingredient for lasting success in the decades to come.

The companies that are succeeding these days are those who have already stopped trying to manipulate us according to the old Middle-Ages-of-Marketing rules. Instead, they are creating shared value with us through the new rules of the Relationship Renaissance. These are the companies that present themselves as human. They are responding to our natural desires for honest and direct relationships, reflecting the character of all commercial relationships prior to industrialization.

This new, more intimate way of relating to customers often bumps up against the traditional values of older established firms. In early 2008, the cofounders of Honest Tea, a small socially and environmentally conscious beverage company, took the controversial step of selling a 40-percent share of their company to Coca-Cola. Seth Goldman and Barry Nalebuff made the move in hope of growing Honest Tea through Coke's superior distribution network. However, before long the two companies differed on an important issue: the wording on the company's Honest Kids package labels.

The terms of sale with Coke allowed Honest Tea to retain control over all its products. But soon after the deal was closed, Coke officials asked Honest Tea to alter the wording on its Honest Kids juice drinks packaging that promised "no high-fructose corn syrup." The New York Times would later write that Coke executives "construed the phrase as an implicit rebuke of its products, some of which contained the controversial factory-produced syrup."[15]

According to the Times, Coke proposed that the anti-syrup wording be either eliminated or changed to "Sweetened with organic cane sugar" or "No fake stuff." Goldman flew down to Atlanta to hash out the issue with his new partners. He had to explain to Coke officials that the message "no high-fructose corn syrup" was important to parents who wanted explicit reassurance that the syrup was not in Honest Tea products.

In March of 2011, Coke bought a majority stake in the company, and the labels on Honest Kids packaging still say "No high-fructose corn syrup."

"Honesty and transparency really is fundamental to the brand," says Peter Kaye, Honest Tea's vice-president of marketing. "Most of our marketing is very straightforward and direct. We sample a lot, enabling us to have a direct conversation with consumers about our ingredients. And when we do advertise it's similarly very direct and straightforward, letting consumers know about the simple, delicious, organic ingredients used in our recipes."[16] At a time when consumer distrust of major institutions, like big corporations and government, is at an all-time high, Honest Tea through its focus on transparency and direct style has built a strong and growing base of loyal consumers.

In some circles, there is the perception that new media and social networks are pushing us into a complex and unfamiliar future where traditional notions of customer loyalty no longer apply. But organizations of all kinds have a lot to learn from the examples of Verizon, Honest Tea, and many others. The Relationship Renaissance requires all businesses, large and small, to learn how to build relationships based on instant karma, in the natural and spontaneous ways by which people have always perceived, judged, helped, and befriended others.

Once you become familiar the ideas in this book, you will start to see everything around you in a different light. You may even come to realize that we've made understanding the world around us much more difficult than it needs to be. It seems that every week there's a new theory and explanation of how the world works—or doesn't work. The best of these ideas have substantial elements of truth to them, but where is the logic in how they all fit together? From Maslow's hierarchy of needs to the psychology of persuasion, from to the innovator's dilemma to emotional intelligence, from Level 5 leadership to conscious capitalism—what is the unifying principle that might put all of these great ideas to work for a better tomorrow? The answer is warmth and competence.

The unchanging compass to our success in the future lies buried deep in our past. It has been obscured by 150 years of industrialization that has fostered an *overreliance* on measures of competence at the expense of warmth, of more genuine concern for others. The revolutions in digital, mobile, and social technologies are taking us back to the way the human species has always prospered, from intimate relationships built on trust and loyalty. We have always been driven more by warmth than by competence in all of our human interactions. The sooner we gain a better grasp of the social science behind this simple truth, the better off we all will be.

With a deeper, fuller understanding of how warmth and competence affect us all, you'll understand better how you are perceived, and you may even expect better of the people in your life, including those who stand behind the products and services you buy. Your primal genius at detecting warmth and competence is a precious gift from your ancestors. Use the following pages as an owner's manual of sorts, one that sheds new light on how and why we make the choices we do.

Chapter One

Warmth and Competence

The two timeless judgments that drive our behavior toward others

During the summer of 2012, Theresa Cook, age eighty-four, was dying of pancreatic cancer in a hospital in Nashua, New Hampshire. Her twenty-one-year-old grandson Brandon was at Theresa's bedside, feeling helpless because she had lost her appetite, and the hospital food didn't appeal to her. What she would really like, she told Brandon, was her favorite food: clam chowder in a bread bowl from the local Panera Bread shop.

It was a Tuesday, and when Brandon called over to Panera on Amherst Street, he discovered that during the summer they made clam chowder only on Fridays. Brandon said he didn't think his grandmother could wait. In three days, she might not be able to eat at all. Suzanne Fortier, the manager of the Nashua Panera, got on the phone, and without missing a beat, asked him to come right over. She told her staff about the special request, and they got to work pulling out the fixings and putting a pot of clam chowder on the stove. By the time Brandon arrived from the hospital, his order had been bagged up, along with a box of cookies for Brandon. Suzanne told Brandon there was no charge and to keep her posted. If his grandmother needed more soup, she said, he should just give a call.

Brandon went home that day and posted a status update to his Facebook friends. He gave a brief account of Suzanne Fortier's and her staff's kindness toward him and his grandmother. Then his mom reposted his update to *her* friends—but she also tagged Panera's corporate page, as well. Within days, Brandon's Facebook post had racked up 730,000 likes and drawn 24,000 comments. Many commenters jumped to conclusions about Panera—positive conclusions of a kind you'd love to see if you were a Panera executive or franchisee:

> "Panera seems like a wonderful company."
> "Glad to hear that there are folks out there that still care for their neighbors and community . . ."
> "CHEERS TO PANERA for following the 'Golden Rule.' Do unto others as you would have them do unto you— and a little kindness goes a long way—there shall be showers of Blessings on this business."
> "Bravo to Panera Bread! Goodness in food, and goodness in people!"
> "What a great story, I have never heard of Panera but I will be sure to try the first one I come across. It's awesome to see how far a little kindness can go."

Many of the online comments reflected the forgone conclusion that Panera Bread was responsible for this act of generosity, but that wasn't really the case. During the ensuing media coverage, Suzanne Fortier explained to interviewers that she'd only done what she felt was decent and right. As the mother of three sons, one of them Brandon's age, she explained that she was impressed by young man's devotion to his grandmother, and she wanted to help.

We make such leaps of logic, attributing the actions of a Panera manager to Panera the company, as an extension of our gift for detecting warmth and competence in others. Research shows that people will judge a single act of generosity as evidence of a generous personality, simply as an effortless, routine by-product of categorizing the act itself as being generous. From the moment of observing someone's single action to inferring that person's seeming personality, we just "know," and we don't even think about how we know.[1]

However, the thoughtful initiative Fortier showed that day happens to be encouraged by Panera's culture. When it comes to community and relationship building, Panera Bread truly is an exceptional company. It was the first national restaurant chain to make a policy of taking end-of-day baked goods to food banks and homeless shelters. It was the first to offer its customers free and open Wi-Fi access. It was also the first chain to put the calorie counts of all its foods on its menus. None of these steps have caused Panera to sacrifice profits. Instead, these measures taken with its customers' interests in mind have helped make Panera the most successful restaurant chain in the first decade of the new millennium. Between 2000 and 2010, Panera outperformed every other stock in the Russell 1000.[2] It's one of those brands that has done well by doing good.

The reason that the story of Suzanne Fortier and Panera Bread went viral online is that we have a spontaneous and immediate attraction to signs of warmth and competence in others. Warmth and competence judgments prompt us to feel friendly toward some and alienated by others. Warmth and competence judgments explain why some inspire our loyalty while others provoke only feelings of suspicion.

Decades of social science research have shown that within the two broad categories of warmth and competence perception, detailed dimensions of how we perceive others can be measured and interpreted to reveal the predictable patterns of emotions and behaviors that result from them. Warmth is judged by assessing whether one is kind, friendly, and good-natured; whether one appears sincere, honest, moral, and trustworthy; and whether one possesses an accommodating orientation and is perceived as helpful, tolerant, fair, generous, and understanding.

Next, we assess people's overall level of competence to understand how successful they would be in carrying out their intentions towards us. Are they stronger or weaker than I am? How much status do they possess? What special resources do they have that make them capable of helping or hurting me? Competence is judged by assessing whether one possesses special resources, skills, creativity, or intelligence that grants them an advantage. Do they appear efficient, capable, skillful, clever, and knowledgeable? Do they seem to possess the confidence and ability to carry out their plans?

These judgments are a remarkably simple but powerful mode of social perception that, by some measures, influences more than 80 percent of all human social behavior. We use warmth and competence to assess not just people, but *everything* in our lives that acts or seems to act of its own free will. So we make warmth and competence judgments about people, groups of people, pets, animal species, teams, companies, brands, and nations. And when the car sometimes "acts up" or when the computer seems to have a mind of its own, we even make warmth and competence judgments about inanimate objects.

Recall the times you have walked down a dark street as a shadowy figure approaches from far off. Your senses immediately go on alert to detect the stranger's intentions toward you. Does the stranger look at you? Is it a casual glance, indicating no threat? Or is it a stare, ambiguous in intent? Just as our ancient ancestors did, you need to judge instantly with imperfect information whether this person intends you well or ill. These immediate judgments of intent assess the stranger's warmth (apparent friendliness or trustworthiness) or its absence. Your reaction, based on this judgment, can be a matter of life or death.

At this same moment, you must also judge how well the stranger can act upon this apparent warm or cold intent you've detected. Is the stranger large or small? Young or old? Male or female? Walking with a swagger or with a limp? Is that a weapon in the stranger's hand or just a bag of groceries? The stranger's apparent competence—the ability to act on intentions—determines how seriously you need to consider your assessment of those intentions.

These two perceptual dimensions, of warmth and competence, are basic to our humanity.[3] To survive and thrive long enough to grow up and have children of their own, our distant ancestors had to judge the intentions and abilities of others quickly and with adequate accuracy to avoid danger. But they also needed to infer with some reliability the warm intent and competent abilities of others, in order to build the relationships necessary to access food, clothing, shelter, and protection offered by tribe or alliance—all of which are just as critical to survival.

Studies show that of the two dimensions, warmth comes earliest and carries more weight in our perceptions. We are highly sensitive to warmth and its absence. Studies show, for example, that you are judged for your trustworthiness within a split second of someone's seeing your face. Moments later, you'll be judged for your competence.[4] Even seemingly minor comments, actions, or appearances can suggest negative intentions that set off emotional alarm bells heard only in the unconscious.

Warm implies trustworthy. Rightly or wrongly, we judge other people's trustworthiness after seeing their faces for a fraction of a second, in the blink of an eye.[5] Imagine someone wide-eyed, with a hint of a smile: the picture of innocence. People with slightly surprised, happy faces and baby-faced people tend to gain our trust almost immediately.[6] Conversely, we immediately distrust people with furrowed brows or frowning, angry faces, judging them cautiously and with suspicion.

Our judgments of competence arrive a fraction of a second more slowly, in maybe two eye-blinks. People with strong, dominant faces tend to win our immediate respect as competent (whether they are or not), and we conversely assume that people who look weak and submissive are actually incompetent, no mat- ter the objective truth. Snap competence judgments of this kind can even predict election outcomes. Research participants shown photos of unfamiliar out-of-state political candidates were able to pick out the winners on the basis of assumed competence two- thirds of the time.[7]

The human face was, in a sense, the first "brand logo"—a rough visual representation of the person's general demeanor in terms of warmth and competence. Our abilities to make these judgments develop so early in life that even babies are able to recognize which puppets and animated characters have good or bad intentions and are able to act competently.[8] Perception of warmth, in particular, predates verbal communication. Consider how parents comfort infants by holding them close. Even baby orphaned monkeys prefer a warm surrogate "mother" fixture blan- keted and warmed by a light bulb, compared to a cold wire-mesh mother, despite the wire-mesh mother's providing a feeding bot- tle. The baby monkeys would rather be warm than fed.[9]

We are so profoundly attracted to warm feelings that social acceptance makes people *feel* physically warmer, while rejection makes them feel colder.[10] Test subjects holding warm beverages behave more generously toward strangers than when they are holding cold beverages.[11]

Research suggests that competence also has bodily manifes- tations. Taller candidates routinely win presidential elections.[12] People who are literally higher up seem like leaders.[13] People who take up space dominate people who take up less space,[14] as do people making fists.[15] Standing strong—"power posing"—raises testosterone, lowers the stress hormone cortisol, and emboldens decision making.[16] (Try this before the job interview, but not dur- ing.) All such larger-than-life physical stances effectively convey dominance, status, and competence to others.

Over a period of decades, social psychologists have identified the warmth dimension by a variety of names such as morality, communality, and "social good-bad." Social psychologists also measure the warmth dimension by asking test subjects to rate other individuals or groups on the basis of perceived traits such as *warm, friendly, likeable, trustworthy, honest,* and *sincere.*[17] Regardless of the specific terms, all are consistent with warm, worthy intentions.

Likewise, psychologists have identified the competence dimension variously as "capability," "agency," and "task good-bad."[18] Perceptions of competence can be measured by asking test subjects to rate individuals and groups for traits such as *capable, intelligent,* and *skilled,* all of which pertain to the ability to act on intentions.

The fundamental dimensions of warmth and competence make the most sense when they are combined to reflect distinctive sets of emotions and behavioral responses. Each combined pattern of warmth and competence perceptions leads to a predictable set of human emotions, and those emotions stimulate a predictable pattern of behavior, as illustrated in Figure 1.1.

Susan began her academic career studying this body of classic person-perception research and then went on to study how we categorize people into social groups by gender, age, ethnicity, and social class. For example, career women, rich people, and highly successful minority groups are often perceived by society

Figure 1.1. The Warmth and Competence Model

Warmth Assessment		Competence Assessment	Emotional Response		Behavioral Response
Warm	+	Competent	→ Admiration, Pride	→	Attraction, Affiliation Alliance
Cold	+	Competent	→ Envy, Jealousy	→	Obligatory Association, Potential Sabotage
Warm	+	Incompetent	→ Sympathy, Pity	→	Patronizing Help, Social Neglect
Cold	+	Incompetent	→ Contempt, Disgust	→	Rejection, Avoidance

at large as being competent but cold; therefore they are envied and begrudged. Disabled people and the elderly are pitied and neglected because they are considered to be warm but incompetent. Research reveals that homeless people, drug addicts, and welfare recipients elicit feelings of contempt and disgust in other people, providing evidence that society rejects such people as being both cold and incompetent. Only groups that reflect the American society's "in-group" ideal picture of itself, such as "middle class" and "citizens," are judged by most people to be admirable for being both warm and competent.

Investigations of these patterns led Susan, along with Amy Cuddy and Peter Glick, to propose the "stereotype content model (SCM)" and the "BIAS (behaviors from intergroup affect and stereotypes) map" by which individual members of society are judged by the majority according to the perception of their respective group's warmth and competence.[19] Dozens of studies in other countries using this model have shown similar patterns of warmth and competence judgments.[20] "Out-groups" judged as incompetent and cold are despised by the majority in every society. Successful and highly competent "out-groups," such as rich people and entrepreneurial minorities, are also judged as "cold," and therefore are commonly treated with envy and suspicion.

Figure 1.2.   Stereotype Content Model (SCM)

	Low Competence	High Competence
High Warmth	Older, disabled **Pity**	In-group, allies, middle class **Pride**
Low Warmth	Poor, homeless, immigrants **Disgust**	Rich, professionals **Envy**

Some of society's darkest and most powerful forces—gender bias, prejudice, ethnic bigotry, and discrimination—rely on the same spontaneous survival mechanism that prompts us to make snap judgments about individuals.[21] In her book *Envy Up, Scorn Down*, Susan points out, however, that although prejudice is hardwired into human nature, acting on it remains a matter of personal choice. The challenge is to come to terms with these primal forces that guide our snap judgments, and then push past them in order to know other people as individuals, not stereotypes. "Solutions," Susan writes, "focus on warmth."[22]

Brands Are People Too

For Chris, all the academic literature on warmth and competence served to confirm many of the concerns he had developed over two decades of researching customer behavior and brand marketing. Chris had long considered traditional brand management principles and practices as unnecessarily complicated and abstract. With the warmth and competence model, he saw a simpler and more direct way to measure our perceptions as customers—a method based on social science and grounded in the fundamental way that people spontaneously perceive, respond to, and judge the world around them.

Consider first that every corporation is literally a body (*corpus*), and as customers, we perceive them as acting with intention and volition, just as we perceive other people. Human psychology has encoded in us the imperative to be wary of others, but also the sense that they have warm intentions toward us and might offer us something of value. Out of our need to secure access to resources, we perceive, judge, and trade with brands and companies just as our most distant ancestors did with people and social groups. To be human is to balance these conflicting impulses—to be on guard and to cooperate.

All of this stands to reason, but prior to 2010 it had never been scientifically tested. Leading marketing academics had proposed related ideas. Susan Fournier and Jennifer Aaker had posited that people have personal brand relationships, with their own ups and downs.[23] Others have described the emotional side of brand relationships.[24] Along with our colleague Nico Kervyn, we set out to test the extent to which warmth and competence insights could be adapted and applied to study customer dynamics.

Susan and Chris's first collaborative study was launched in June 2010, during a period when several of America's best-known companies and brands were embroiled in unprecedented public relations turmoil. In the winter and spring of 2009–2010, the venerated Tylenol brand and its parent Johnson & Johnson were clumsily struggling through a series of embarrassing product recalls. The McNeil Consumer Healthcare unit initiated a string of ever-widening product recalls that included Tylenol Arthritis Pain Caplets, Benadryl, Motrin, Rolaids, Simply Sleep, St. Joseph Aspirin, Tylenol, and more than forty types of children's and infants' products. By May 2010, the FDA had shuttered the primary manufacturing plant for Tylenol products in North America due to poor sanitary conditions and safety standard violations.

Around the same time, BP, the third-largest energy company in the world, was trying in vain to plug an undersea oil gusher created by the April 2010 explosion of the Deepwater Horizon oil rig, which killed eleven workers. While this was under way, we asked one thousand U.S. adults to evaluate BP, Tylenol, and six other widely known companies and brands—Shell, Advil, McDonald's, Burger King, Tropicana, and Minute Maid. The objective was to quantify the extent to which warmth and competence influenced the behavior of customers, and to see how these crises had affected public perceptions of these companies and brands.

The findings were startling; they showed that companies and brands were judged so strongly along the lines of warmth and competence dimensions that these judgments explained nearly 50 percent of all purchase intent, loyalty, and likelihood to recommend a brand or company. To put that 50 percent figure in perspective, consumer research is normally considered to be significant if it reveals a new variable explaining as little as 15 percent of customer behavior.

The customers in our study showed widespread distrust for BP and reported a low rate of purchase intent and brand loyalty for BP locations, about 40 percent lower than for Shell stations. The results for Tylenol, however, showed that the brand was largely unharmed by the bad publicity surrounding its product recalls and FDA actions. Tylenol scored twice as high as BP on such warmth characteristics as "honest and trustworthy" and "acts in the customer's best interests." In fact, customers reported substantially higher purchase intent and brand loyalty for Tylenol than for its competitor, Advil, even though the Advil brand had enjoyed a blemish-free record.

Customers appeared to have interpreted Tylenol's production problems to be a short-term, forgivable lapse in competence that did not impair its reputation for warm intentions. Tylenol's maker, Johnson & Johnson, has long acted on a companywide credo that directs employees to put customers first. The company's behavior in the face of Tylenol product-tampering deaths in 1982 became a textbook case of effective crisis management. McNeil Consumer Healthcare eventually took the same extraordinary and selfless actions J&J had become known for in 1982. After a stinging FDA report on poor production conditions at its main Tylenol production plant in Pennsylvania, McNeil voluntarily shut the plant for retooling, effectively removing Tylenol from store shelves and costing the company hundreds of millions of dollars. Through the parent company's willingness to take large financial hit and go far beyond what the situation required, Tylenol retained the trust of consumers.

BP, in contrast, had led with defensive words instead of selfless actions when the Deepwater Horizon blew up and sank in the Gulf of Mexico. BP spokespeople laid blame with the rig's owner and sought to minimize the extent of the oil spill. CEO

Tony Hayward insisted that the environmental impact would be "very, very modest." He pleaded ignorance of the company's operations and deflected responsibility in Congressional testimony. Underwater cameras recorded in real time the company's failures to staunch the gusher of oil polluting the gulf, cementing the image of BP as fundamentally incompetent. And with a record of recent safety failures that included a deadly refinery explosion in 2005 and an Alaskan oil spill in 2006, BP had no store of goodwill on which to draw.

A key element of Chris and Susan's work together is how perceptions like these become reality in the public mind. The research explores how we talk about the companies and brands we buy from: "My cable company doesn't respect my time." "My insurance company hates me." "My computer loves me." A peer-reviewed, academic study subsequently showed how warmth and competence dimensions drive people's purchase and loyalty behavior.[25]

The study, involving well-known companies, showed recognizable clusters of brands spread out across the intentions-and-ability matrix (see Figure 1.3). The most popular brands—Hershey's, Johnson & Johnson, Campbell's, and Coca-Cola—all landed in the well-intentioned, capable quadrant of high warmth and high competence. People admired them, said they would purchase from them, and expressed loyalty to them.

Troubled brands—which included BP, AIG, Goldman Sachs, and Marlboro—all rated as low on ability and low on intentions. People expressed neither planned purchase nor expected loyalty. These brands landed in the "contempt and disgust" quadrant, ranking low on both warmth and competence.

Luxury brands—Mercedes, Porsche, Rolls Royce, and Rolex—rated high on ability but tended to score low on good intentions. People reported feeling envy toward these as a result of their ability to enact their intentions. Both dimensions strongly predicted purchase and loyalty behavior.

Figure 1.3.   Brand Warmth-and-Competence Matrix

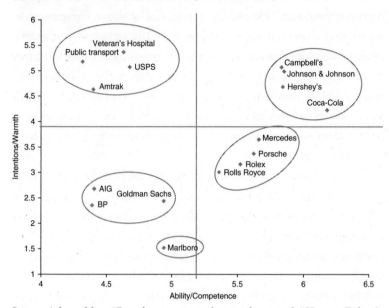

Source: Adapted from "Brands as intentional agents framework," Kervyn, Fiske, & Malone, *Journal of Consumer Psychology,* April 2012.

Finally, government-subsidized corporations fell into the region of sympathetic and pitied brands. The U.S. Postal Service, Veteran's Administration hospitals, Amtrak, and public transportation agencies were all regarded as well-intended but incompetent. Again, both dimensions predicted purchase and loyalty—their intentions ranked positively but perceptions of competence were low.

The research confirmed that customers reward perceptions of warmth and competence with feelings of admiration, purchases, and customer loyalty. Just as we all assess other human beings, we also assess the intentions and abilities of companies and brands. Perceptions of a company's intentions and abilities trigger specific customer emotions, which in turn drive customer behavior. Companies and brands win our affiliation and loyalty just as real people do, by worthy intentions and capability, through warmth and competence.

A larger follow-up research project, focused on chocolate manufacturer Hershey in 2011, helped illuminate the extent to which customer loyalty is enhanced by the perception of warm intentions in particular. In this study, customers rated Hershey higher on warmth and competence than any of the other twenty-six companies studied to that point. And yet, few of Hershey's customers are aware that the majority ownership of Hershey's is in the hands of a philanthropic charitable trust. The majority of Hershey profits are devoted to funding the Milton Hershey School in Pennsylvania, the nation's largest boarding school for underprivileged children.

The research was designed to test the hypothesis that customers would view philanthropic efforts by a particular brand or company as a reflection of the warmth and competence of the people leading that brand. The question was whether customers would internalize those perceptions as an indicator of what they could expect in their own dealings with that brand or company, and whether those perceptions would in turn increase brand loyalty.

Because Hershey's philanthropy isn't widely known, it provided an ideal test case among a demographically representative sample of U.S. customers. First the research captured the participants' brand perceptions, purchase intent, and loyalty toward Hershey. Then the participants were exposed to the story of the Hershey Trust's funding of the Milton Hershey School. They were questioned about their prior awareness of these charitable efforts and how this information impacted their views on the brand and company. Finally, they were asked once again about their perceptions, purchase intent, and loyalty toward Hershey.

As expected, very few customers were aware of Hershey's philanthropic roots, and nearly 80 percent of respondents indicated that their views of the Hershey Company and its employees and products were more favorable once they were aware of the story. The respondents reported more favorable perceptions of the Hershey brand across all warmth, competence, and social

Figure 1.4.   Impact of Hershey Philanthropy Awareness

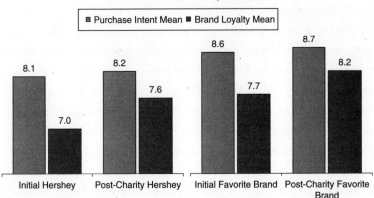

On a scale from 1 to 10, again please indicate: how likely you would be to make a purchase of/how strong and loyal a preference you feel for Hershey when you have a need for chocolate products?

■ Purchase Intent Mean ■ Brand Loyalty Mean

responsibility measures. Customers apparently conclude that Hershey's charitable heritage also indicates that the brand acts fairly toward its customers, employees, dairy farmer suppliers, and communities as well.

The Hershey's research results show how, in the mind of the customer, a company's people *are*, in fact, the primary basis of judgment. Customer loyalty and purchase intent were strongly influenced by what customers knew about the real people behind Hershey's, despite an already high baseline level for the brand. Just as important, the research showed how specific information about the intentions and behavior of the people behind companies and brands can significantly affect customer perceptions and loyalty to the products and services those people produce—even while the product itself remains unchanged.

To test this idea further, Susan and Chris performed another study in which one group of U.S. adults read about a hypothetical company "seen as consistently acting with the public's best interests in mind and having good intentions toward ordinary people." Another group read about a hypothetical company with the opposite traits, described as able or not: "(un)skilled and (in)effective" and "having (lacking) the ability to imple-ment its intentions." Participants then rated the company on its warmth and competence, the emotions it aroused, and their own likely reactions.

Participants rewarded the well-intentioned, capable com-pany with high ratings on warmth and competence, admiration, purchase intent, and loyalty. They punished the ill-intentioned, incapable company with low ratings on warmth and competence, higher contempt, and lower purchase and loyalty. The mixed companies mostly received appropriately mixed reactions.

For Ed Martin, Hershey's director of international insights and new methods, these results offered him the ability for the first time to quantify the value of corporate social responsibility efforts for brand and company business results. As a self-described "believer in conscious capitalism and purposeful business," Ed wanted to make those findings available to the larger philan-thropic community in support of efforts to encourage corporate social responsibility. Since the study, Hershey has expanded its philanthropic activities and has also become more willing to talk about them.

We shared the details of our findings with McNeil, and the company used our study to articulate in internal meetings pre-cisely how they differed from findings about companies and brands that had seen significant decreases in customer loyalty and purchase intent following recalls. McNeil then commis-sioned a deeper study, conducted in April-May 2011, designed in part to determine how warmth and competence insights might greatly accelerate Tylenol's recovery upon its planned relaunch in the market.

The Language of Loyalty

The Coca-Cola Company employs a sophisticated brand equity model to measure and track the strength of its connections to customers through market research in over two hundred countries. The company has used these tools to predict customer behavior, and identify areas requiring improvement to generate purchase and loyalty growth. However, Coca-Cola consumption had been steadily slipping for the past few years, even though all of the measures of brand health tracked remained relatively stable. Chris worked with Coca-Cola's vice president for marketing strategy & insights, Stan Sthanunathan, and its director of marketing research, Clare Hulsey, to add warmth and competence dimensions to the company's model; they then analyzed the results extensively.

The company's existing model explained nearly 50 percent of customer behavior—a very good batting average, as any marketing researcher would tell you. But the addition of warmth and competence dimensions increased the model's explanatory power to 58 percent. When the results were examined in greater detail, however, a curious pattern emerged. The warmth and competence model was much more effective in identifying loyalty behavior among Coca-Cola's most passionately committed customers. Moving up Coca-Cola's customer loyalty hierarchy, from casual purchasers to fanatical supporters, the existing model's predictive strength went down dramatically, while the predictive strength of warmth and competence went up. Coca-Cola's existing brand health model was least accurate with the company's most loyal and valuable customers. For its most loyal customers, the warmth and competence dimensions improved the predictive validity of Coca-Cola's brand equity model by 146 percent.

This result provided us with a very valuable insight: the stronger the relationship between Coca-Cola and a customer, the more closely that relationship resembles a one-on-one human relationship in terms of warmth and competence.

All this research suggests that if companies are going to succeed with customers in the Relationship Renaissance, a new language of loyalty is needed, one built around warmth and competence.

Figure 1.5. Coca-Cola Purchase Intent Explained at Differing Loyalty Levels

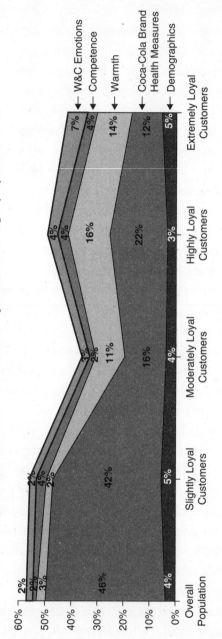

Our loyalty as customers doesn't commit us to abstract companies or brands. Rather, we become loyal to what we experience, learn, or infer about the intentions of people behind those companies and brands. And we don't even need to know those people first-hand. Related research on computers and websites as "social agents" shows that we rely on warmth and competence even when engaging in commerce online. Computers easily gain personalities, and test subjects act politely toward computers they interact with.[26] We exercise politeness toward websites,[27] consistent with the idea that we humanize our technology, just as we humanize our contacts with brands and companies.

Taken together, these findings suggest that people were likely the first "brands" and human faces perhaps the first "logos," meaning that all the branded trade and commerce that has unfolded over the past several thousand years is simply our adaptive response to a civilized world in which we enjoy the benefits of products and services made by "unseen hands." Our mental apparatus perceives brands as stand-ins for people, logos as substitutes for faces, and companies as the equivalent of a tribe or social group. Accordingly, we perceive, judge, and interact with everything in our world in the way we have evolved to interact with other humans.

We all inherently know that a bottle of Coca-Cola is an inanimate object. But we also know it is produced by a company and that the company is made up of people. And despite the fact that we may not have any direct contact with any of those people, we can infer insights about them from Coca-Cola's packaging, its product's quality, the things we hear from others, and our first-hand experience with the product. And as the Hershey study showed, the more we find out about the intentions and abilities of the people behind the product, the more likely we are to become their loyal customers. To that extent, the best companies and brands, the ones we bond with, are those that we are most easily able to relate to and evaluate on the basis of their human characteristics.

This insight, profound in its implications, runs counter to how companies and brands have been managed for the past fifty years. If we perceive, judge, and become loyal to companies and brands using the same warmth and competence thought processes we use to form relationships with other people, it appears that companies have been pursuing customer loyalty on the basis of a number of mistaken premises.

For instance, conventional wisdom in the business world tells us that customer loyalty is synonymous with repeat patronage. Loyalty, by this reasoning, is simply the continued purchase of a product or service over a particular period of time, regardless of how and why it happens. Our studies suggest, however, that purchase behavior by itself is a poor indicator of whether customers have strong and loyal relationships with companies and brands. In fact, our research suggests that continued patronage and genuine customer loyalty are two entirely different things.

Why are Tylenol customers more loyal than Advil customers? What motivates increased loyalty in Hershey's buyers? What is the basis of brand loyalty among Coca-Cola's most ardent fans? None of these questions can be answered by measuring repeat patronage. They can be satisfied only through the lens of warmth and competence.

These findings, along with the rise of the Relationship Renaissance, call for a new approach by businesses, one that seeks to build trust-based relationships with us as their customers. They need to demonstrate a lasting commitment to us before they can expect our commitment to them in terms of repeat purchases. The very definition and language of customer loyalty needs to be rethought. It needs to reflect not how loyal and committed customers are to companies and brands, but rather how loyal and committed are they to us.

Chapter Two

The Loyalty Test

*Why we expect companies and
brands to commit to us first*

Pretend for a moment that you work in the procurement
department of a large hospital. Over your morning coffee, you notice a *Wall Street Journal* story about the company
that sells you dressings and bandages. Profits at the company
doubled in the previous quarter, and the stock price rose by
8 percent to $39 per share.

You might consider this nice news, because this same medical
supply company is one of the vendors you use. But you also know
first-hand what's really behind that glowing profit report. For
the past two years, this company has been trimming its payrolls
to please Wall Street, and your service has suffered as a result.
Billing mistakes have popped up frequently, and they have taken
a lot of effort to rectify. Frank, your harried and overworked sales
rep, has become increasingly hard to reach. You try to use their
web portal to investigate and resolve your billing issues, but the
interface is slow and balky. In fact, if you didn't feel just a little
sorry for Frank, you likely would have switched your account to
another medical products supplier long ago. And that's why you

don't feel particularly happy for Frank's company. If anything, you feel a little resentful and exploited, as if the company had beat its Wall Street expectations partly at your expense, and without so much as a word of thanks for your loyalty through tough times.

Large, publicly traded companies often choose to make favorable impressions on the investment community by behaving toward customers, to put it in relationship terms, like classic gold-diggers. Gold-diggers pretend to be interested in you, but all they really want is your money. Yes, we expect the companies we buy from to make profits and look out for themselves. We want them to stay healthy, so they'll be there for us tomorrow. But we expect them to look out for us, too, if only to preserve our goodwill and patronage. When they seem to shortchange us for their own benefit, we feel they are cold and exploitative.

"Warmth," as we've seen, is a word that can be used to describe a wide array of admirable qualities, but they all add up to a reliable, trustworthy concern for others. Social psychologists note that warmth benefits others, while competence benefits the self.[1] A person who is honest, reliable, and agreeable demonstrates warmth by demonstrating concern for other people's interests and needs, even if the person might gain more in the short term from doing otherwise.

The same goes for companies. Companies that exercise genuine warmth exhibit a willingness to respond sincerely to their customers' needs, even at their own short-term expense. The most-admired ones tend to be those that establish trusting, long-term relationships with their customers by making it a point to put customers first and themselves second. For instance, the Nordstrom's department store chain offers such legendary customer service that it has been known to take back a dress that no longer fits because the owner has gained weight. That's an extreme example of a commitment to the needs of others. That's authentic warmth—and loyalty to the customer.

If that also seems like a foolhardy and unprofitable way to run a business, consider how costly it is to operate with a more transactional orientation, with a sharp focus on short-term sales and profits. Companies and brands that seek quick and impersonal transactions with us tempt us to leave them every day. They may be highly competent and efficient, but by acting in direct defiance of our need for warmth, they trigger our natural feelings of suspicion and distrust. If they lack warmth and offer little sense of their loyalty to us, these companies naturally leave us cold. Having failed to earn our loyalty, they are forced to go on endless and expensive hunts for new customers to replace the ones they keep frustrating and losing. They are like the regulars at a monthly speed-dating event. Eventually, word gets around about what they're really interested in.

Social psychologists recognize this distinction, too, as a "communal" versus an "exchange" relationship.[2] The rules in an exchange relationship are tit-for-tat; you scratch my back, and I'll scratch yours. People in exchange relationships keep track of what they are giving and getting. Your officemate borrows money and then returns it. The sandwich shop gives you what you ordered for the agreed price. You get back according to what you put in.

By contrast, the rules in a communal relationship rely on responsiveness to each other's needs; we take care of each other. We are in it together, so people in communal relationships keep track of each other's wishes, not their input. If your neighbor borrows a cup of sugar, you would be more pleased to get back some of the resulting cookies than a precisely calibrated cup of sugar. A lunch date that ends with "Let me buy you the exact same lunch here tomorrow" seems weird and less friendly that one that ends, "That was fun! I know this great place for a drink after work; I think you'd like it, if you are free later this week." Communal relationships consider the other's needs and interests, rather than trying to even the score.

No business can afford to operate on strictly communal basis, but by introducing a healthy mix of communality to its regular exchange transactions, a company can create relationships that pay off for both the company and its customers in the long term. Also, rational self-interest and generous other-interest need not be a trade-off. Psychologists show that these two qualities function independently of each other, so people and companies can rank high on both self-interest and other-interest in their relationships.[3]

If we do relate to businesses the way we relate to other people, then demonstrating the warmth of communality creates more trust in the long term than the cold calculation of exchange transactions. In essence, we unconsciously conduct a loyalty test as we assess the warmth and competence of a person, a company, or a brand. We make a series of fast calculations (which are demonstrated at LoyaltyTest.com) in relation to the categories of warmth and competence that heavily influence our willingness to extend our loyalty.

Dropped Calls

For much of the early 2000s, Nextel enjoyed the highest customer satisfaction rankings and highest rates of customer loyalty among all its U.S. wireless competitors. In many industries, including the building trades, Nextel was the must-have carrier, thanks to a unique push-to-talk feature in its network, which allowed users to connect with each other instantly, using their phones as walkie-talkies. The telltale chirp of Nextel push-to-talk ringers led one business writer to observe in 2005 that "lots of construction sites sound like bird sanctuaries."[4]

That year, Nextel was bought out by its rival Sprint for $35 billion. The move was greeted as good news by shareholders, because the purchase allowed the merged "Sprint Nextel" to step up as the nation's third-largest wireless company. For Nextel subscribers, though, the news was not so good. Sprint and Nextel phones operated on separate, incompatible networks, and as soon as Nextel was absorbed into Sprint, Nextel's network began to suffer.

One Nextel subscriber complained, "On my twenty-minute drive to and from work every day, I'd lose a call up to five times . . . This never happened before the Sprint-Nextel merger." In less than a year, a full-blown exodus had begun, with hundreds of thousands of traditionally loyal Nextel subscribers fleeing the newly merged Sprint Nextel. Those locked in to long-term wireless contracts flooded support lines with complaints. How did the company respond? Some frequent callers to support lines had their contracts canceled, with CNET.com reporting: "Sprint breaks up with high-maintenance customers: Wireless carrier sends Dear John letters to customers who it says call the customer support line too often."[5]

By the time Dan Hesse took over as CEO of Sprint in late 2007, losses were running in the billions of dollars each quarter. Sprint had the lowest customer service rating in the industry and one of the highest customer churn rates, nearly double that of AT&T and Verizon. If Sprint customers were unhappy, Hesse determined, it was because within Sprint's management structure there was no accountability for keeping them happy. The *New York Times* reported that in Hesse's first meeting with top executives, "he demanded to know who was responsible for appeasing disgruntled customers. No one raised a hand."[6]

Many of Hesse's first steps to right the ship involved making explicit commitments of loyalty to Sprint's customers. Hesse appeared in television ads inviting current customers to email him directly with their comments and complaints. He asked former customers to give Sprint another chance. Every meeting he headed began with a presentation by his chief service officer. And although Sprint was still facing enormous financial losses, Hesse increased the number of call center employees until there were enough to guarantee that 80 percent of calls were being handled within thirty seconds.

The training and procedures for call center personnel were also reoriented. Previously, when call centers had been understaffed and overwhelmed, managers pressed employees to keep calls short, in order to cut down on waiting time for other callers. There was no pressure, though, to actually resolve the customers' complaints, so customers frequently had to call more than once just to have their problems handled effectively. Under the new regime, Sprint started measuring the rates of "first-call resolution," and for the first time, compensation was tied to customer satisfaction. More calls were steered toward call centers that excelled at first-call resolutions, while Sprint phased out the centers with poorer results.

Harley Manning of Forrester Research said of Sprint in 2010: "There aren't many companies that say they don't care about their customers . . . But actually doing the tactical work to change the organization and culture, such as changing compensation and making one executive accountable for the customer experience, is something different. And Sprint is doing it."[7] That year Forrester named Sprint among the three most-improved companies in its annual Customer Experience survey ranking. Other independent survey groups put Sprint at the top of the wireless industry for customer satisfaction, after it had been at the bottom just two years earlier. Most important, the volume of calls to support centers and the churn rate of fleeing customers both dropped back to industry averages.

"It's not rocket science," Bob Johnson, Sprint's chief service officer, told the *Kansas City Star*, in reference to his call center operations. "When they call us, I am going to do a better job of taking care of them. I am going to take care of your problem. I am going to make you feel good. It will be hard for you to leave." By May 2012, Sprint was again ranked first in customer satisfaction among major wireless carriers by both J.D. Power & Associates and the American Customer Satisfaction Index.[8]

Perhaps the best evidence of Sprint's change of heart on taking care of customers was expressed by one of its frontline employees. "What I preach to all of my team is to treat customers like they're family members," said Alex Alum, a store manager in South Miami Beach. "The better a customer feels when they leave the store, the more referral business they're going to bring to us. And long-lasting relationships come from great customer service."[9] Communal warmth motivates more loyalty than does cold calculation.

No Community but the Investment Community

A lot of public companies never pull out of the kind of death spiral that Sprint had entered in 2007. Once a recession takes a bite out of a company's revenue, Wall Street wants to see layoffs and cost-cutting that will prop up the share price. From the perspective of management, layoffs and spending cuts are survival tactics necessary to remain in the good graces of the investment community. There is little consideration that if staffing is cut and customer relationships get shredded, the company will have less to build on when better economic conditions return a few years down the road.

Pretend again that you're working in that hospital procurement office described at the opening of the chapter. You don't really know what's going on at Frank's company. You just know Frank is harder to reach than he used to be, and that he's not very helpful when you reach him. You spend $2 million a year with Frank's company, and you don't appreciate how you're being treated. There's something very transactional about Frank's attitude, something you've never seen in him before.

The fact is that Frank is now doing his job *and* the job of two other people who have been laid off. So he's had to do the absolute minimum for you, strictly to the letter of his contract. The supplies keep coming, and you keep paying Frank's bills. But there is a limit to the power of mere competence to maintain bonds of loyalty in such a relationship. When a company treats us competently but coldly, we don't feel particularly grateful, even if the service or product provides us with excellent value for the dollar.

Instead, as the research shows, we see a cold and competent company acting in a transactional exchange for its own benefit first, with little thought given to our needs or desires. We feel used.

Competence without warmth is likely to leave us feeling suspicious. It makes us worry that our competent partner might cast aside our needs the minute that it's in that partner's interest to do so. And you would be right to worry. That's what happened to the customers that Sprint "fired" for complaining about Sprint's terrible service.

Unfortunately, the tactic of slashing costs and service levels to preserve cash flow has become commonplace for large corporations struggling through hard times. It's very easy to for management to discount or overlook the extent to which such short-term cuts can alienate customers, increase customer churn, and inevitably reduce long-term profitability. That's because, for the management of most public companies, there is no community more important than the investment community.

A Question of Loyalty

By May 2012, Sprint CEO Dan Hesse was able to boast in an investor conference call how the decision to invest in customer loyalty, besides being the right thing to do, was also proving to be extremely profitable. For two years, Sprint had extended loyalty to its customers in any number of ways throughout its operations, from simplified billing to better call center experiences. The customers responded with loyalty of their own. They stayed, and many paid more for the privilege. Customers showed that if Sprint was willing to improve, they'd be willing to spend a little more to stick with the company.

"Good customer service costs less," Hesse told investors, "and customers will pay more for good service. So it is the ultimate win-win." Hesse estimated that Sprint was able to reduce expenses by $5 billion thanks to the combination of simpler billing and better service. Sprint closed twenty-nine call centers because call volume had dropped. Sprint also saved a lot of money by not having to placate disgruntled customers with credits to their accounts. "We give customers far fewer credits," Hesse explained, "because when a customer is quite frankly ticked off and about to leave, very often you give the customer a credit, satisfy them, or what have you. If you provide good service, you don't need to do that."

The most remarkable news, though, was that once Sprint began to improve its service, the company felt it could at long last raise some prices. The company's average revenue per user went up $4 in the first quarter of 2012, which was, in Hesse's words, "more than any US company has ever done year-over-year in the history of the industry."[10]

Plenty of research shows that companies with high levels of customer retention enjoy higher-than-average profits,[11] but traditionally, companies and brands have wrongly interpreted this to mean that if they can just keep customers, even by bribing them with discounts and perks, then they have loyal long-term customers. Rewarding repeat patronage, however, is not the same thing as offering loyalty first and engendering loyalty in return. Systems of rewards and benefits are really just price cuts and discounts in disguise. And price cuts and discounts, nice as they are, do not inspire loyalty because they have no effect on our enduring, human triggers for warmth.

Frequent Flying

In 2006, by one estimate, the U.S. dollar was quietly replaced as the world's leading circulating currency. The dollar wasn't toppled by the euro or the yen, though. Instead, the number-one global currency was airline frequent-flyer miles. The total stock of unredeemed frequent-flyer miles was estimated at the time to be worth more than $700 billion, which would exceed the value of all the dollar notes and U.S. coins on earth.[12]

What are we getting for this massive investment of resources in the name of customer "loyalty"? Not very much. These so-called loyalty programs suffer from two major flaws that likely cause them to do more harm than good. First, as we all know, they are easily copied and offered by every company and brand in a given category. The differences among competitor programs tend to not be very significant, nor do they last long. So while we may lose a little by spreading our purchases across multiple companies or brands, we can pretty easily switch between them as we like. Because all competitors offer rebates of some kind, we earn rebates from those we choose to, and not much changes in our loyalty to those companies and brands.

Consider, for instance, the basic premise of all the airline, hotel, credit card, and even retailer loyalty programs we join. For every purchase we make, we are given reward points that can be redeemed for free products, services, or cash. And this is reasonably appealing to most of us, because who wouldn't want a rebate or discount on things that we were planning to buy anyway? But let's be clear. This is certainly not relationship-based loyalty to a company or brand that we trust and prefer to patronize. It's a financial rebate or discount for making repeated purchases, whether or not we like and trust the seller.

The worst thing about loyalty and reward programs is that they absolutely, positively result in higher costs for companies— costs passed along to all of us in the form of higher prices. A 2009 study of credit card reward programs by the Federal Reserve Bank of Kansas City concluded that both customers and card issuers are most likely worse off from the proliferation of these programs.[13]

The management of a typical reward program can represent an enormous portion of a company's annual marketing spend. In the hotel industry, once a customer has enrolled in a reward program, a portion of every subsequent purchase (typically about 5 percent) is set aside in an account to fund reward redemptions and other program expenses. From an accounting standpoint, these reward funds are treated a bit like retail bank deposits. A certain reserve level must be maintained at all times to ensure that all rewards redeemed can be paid. An outside actuarial review each year determines the reserve level for the coming year, based on recent activity. This review takes into account the assumption that substantial portions of all reward points will expire before they can be redeemed.

So in addition to the costs of program rewards, lots of additional expenses go into managing, monitoring, and promoting enrollment in these programs. That's where the Kansas City Fed study saw losses to both the provider and the customer. The main beneficiaries seem to be the vast network of service providers that profit from selling and managing these reward programs for companies and brands.

At the root of the problem, again, has been a fundamental misunderstanding of the nature of loyalty, with the belief that genuine, relationship-based customer loyalty can be bought with rebates and rewards. As anyone who has been frustrated with the service provided by their wireless carrier, cable company, or the dominant airline at their nearest airport can attest, our continued purchases are typically not a sign of our loyalty. Rather, they are more often a sign that we are essentially being held hostage, unable to switch to a better alternative without significant negative consequences of some kind.

From the opposite perspective, Wharton professor Stephen Hoch notes that we often feel high levels of loyalty to retailers who have no loyalty or reward programs at all—Trader Joe's being the most prominent example. That observation alone puts the credibility of loyalty and reward programs in doubt.

"A lot of these loyalty programs are just a lame way of giving a heavy user a discount," Hoch said in a 2007 interview. "That's not necessarily bad, because heavy users are more price-sensitive. You want to give them discounts, but the question is, does it create loyalty if everybody is doing the same thing for that heavy user?"[14]

Hoch seems to ask, just how thin can our so-called "loyalty" be spread? Many of us, for instance, have loyalty cards for three or four different supermarkets, which suggests that we're not loyal to any of them. We use loyalty cards just to qualify for discounts wherever we happen to be shopping.

As a general rule, reward programs in the travel industry are designed to maximize customer participation while limiting actual reward redemptions. This frequently involves a promotional advertising campaign that says "earn a free X after just Y" purchases, which generally sounds pretty reasonable and attractive. However, customers often don't realize that there are special requirements and limitations in the fine print of the offer. For instance, there may be extra steps required to become eligible for the offer or limitations on when or where the reward can be redeemed. These all are designed to keep redemptions to a manageable level, because the reserve held for rewards would be quickly overspent if every eligible customer were compensated for every eligible purchase.

Though it may sound odd that these programs are designed to ensure that a significant proportion of earned rewards are never actually delivered to customers. This "slippage," as it is called, is a central component of every reward program in every industry. In fact, when companies and brands implement changes in the terms and conditions of their reward programs, it's often to enable them to better manage the slippage on reward redemption and reduce the liability of earned but unredeemed rewards from their balance sheet. The problem with all of this financial risk management is that lots of customers don't discover the fine-print requirements and limitations until after the purchase. As you can imagine, this does not make for happy and loyal customers.

Despite the heavy investments made in these programs to build and reward loyalty, they often leave customers jaded and indifferent at best or angry and resentful at worst. However, the especially painful truth for companies and brands in industries like airlines, hotels, and credit cards is that the reward programs have become so ubiquitous, expected, and taken for granted by customers, it's no longer possible for them to compete without one—not because they are especially effective, but rather because the most valuable customers won't even consider doing business with them without this industry-standard perk. As a result, they've become a price-of-entry commodity for customers, like the ante to participate in a round of poker. Overall, reward programs do a poor job of maintaining the kind of customer loyalty that is possible naturally when two people get to know and appreciate each other.

Considering how merchants built loyalty with their customers before the Middle Ages of Marketing, we can see some interesting parallels to what reward programs are trying but failing to accomplish today. In a small community, merchants soon noticed which customers they were seeing on a regular basis. They would recognize faces, get to know names, remember shopping habits, and appreciate patronage. Commonly, the merchant might offer a volume discount or throw in a few tokens of that appreciation. Our human nature compels us to reciprocate acts of kindness,[15] and gifts signal the wish for communal relationships. These long-ago merchants were certainly no different from the rest of us in this regard. So although it wasn't until 1896 that the Sperry & Hutchinson Company began offering their S&H Green Stamps program to retailers, the concept of rewarding loyal customers had been employed by merchants for centuries as a gesture of human warmth and appreciation.[16]

Another key aspect of the loyalty that developed between merchants and customers was recognition. Because merchants historically knew customers on a personal basis, they could expect to be greeted by name and perhaps receive a little extra attention as well. This kind of recognition required genuine interest on the merchant's part to remember important customers and then treat them differently when they arrived. Warm behavior of this sort alerts us to another person's caring for us and deserving our loyalty. Worthy intentions also have much greater influence on our loyalty than rewards or discounts do.

Of course, today's reward programs attempt to accomplish something similar by creating multiple status levels to recognize differing levels of patronage. Silver, gold, platinum, or diamond status each offer different privileges, rewards, or service. However, the hotels, airlines, banks, and retailers granting us these privileges don't really recognize us at all. They register only an account number, its associated transactions, and its corresponding rewards. We are often only a number to them. This automated system tries to compensate for our becoming, during the Middle Ages of Marketing, merely nameless, faceless "consumers" with whom they have no actual relationship.

What's more, any special recognition promised with such reward status frequently goes undelivered. Having been assured of special attention, we end up feeling more annoyed and disappointed than if they had offered no reward program in the first place. An executive in the hotel industry tells of his frustration in attempting to deliver rewards recognition and benefits through his chain's network of franchise owners. His chain had instituted a set of new recognition benefits for its "elite status" members, including a complimentary room upgrade, but on his first trip out of town he saw the reality—an uninterested desk clerk ignoring his "elite status" card at check-in, failing to offer a room upgrade, and even showing mildly insulting indifference when the executive pointed out that he was an elite status member. "He couldn't have been more relationship-destroying if he tried," the executive recalls. His chain began investigating how to automate elite status recognition, bypassing the front desk entirely with electronic communications, such as sending welcoming mobile texts at check-in.

More often, reward programs bombard us with email offers roughly based on our prior behavior, with no real knowledge of why we bought or what we did. They push us and overwhelm us with deals and irrelevant suggestions, often alienating us by demonstrating that their main interest is their own sales objectives, not us. Early merchants knew customers well enough to know what they liked, talked about things that were relevant to them, and made them offers based on that knowledge. They kept an eye out for things that might be of interest to their loyal customers, and even when they failed to provide superior service, they at least knew their customers well enough to recognize when they owed appropriate apologies.

Customers who complain about a company but then experience promptness and respect often become more loyal to the company than customers who have had no complaints.[17] The reason goes right to the importance of warmth and loyalty. A complaint sparks an interaction, which in turn provides the opportunity to demonstrate loyalty to the customer. On the other hand, if any number of faceless monoliths favor us with points, miles, and tenth-coffee-free offers, we're happy to have the discounts, but we're not going to feel much in the way of true loyalty.

Wharton marketing professor Erik Clemons points to his own personal example. Almost twenty years ago, he had a miserable stay at the InterContinental Hotel in London. He wrote out a detailed list of everything that had gone wrong during his visit, and then as he was checking out, the guest relations manager went over his complaints with him. She asked him to come back again and give the hotel another chance. From then on, the InterContinental had Clemons' profile down. For example, when he was traveling with his young daughter, the hotel made sure he didn't get a room with a balcony, which could be dangerous. Clemons has stayed in the InterContinental chain dozens of nights a year ever since.

The InterContinental manager who followed up with Clemons says that she flags complainers because "if they care enough to bring it to your attention, then it is important to turn things around for them and turn that to strength. I've followed up on quite a few regular guests who have had problems. They can end up being your most loyal customers."[18] This seeming quirk in human behavior only helps bear out the idea that we are loyal to the people behind companies and brands, not their products, prices, or loyalty programs. As Loyalty Testers, we are usually glad to forgive a failing grade and dispense "extra credit" where it's due.

From Acquaintances to Advocates

Dr. Kelly Faddis operates one of the most unusual dental practices in the United States. Out of a $1.2 million office in the Salt Lake City area, he serves a clientele that includes people who fly in from as far away as Texas and Bermuda. Many of these clients come to him even though he doesn't take their insurance. He doesn't give discounts or run promotions. He doesn't advertise.

You might suspect that Dr. Faddis is an exceptionally competent dentist. He did graduate seventh in his dental class, but he'd say that's not what sets him apart. Rather, Faddis is first and foremost a practitioner of loyalty to his patients. They all have his cell phone number. He books only one patient at a time, so no one ever waits. And he takes a lot of time to educate patients about how they can take of their teeth themselves, increasing what he calls "their dental IQ." His aim is for them to understand their treatment well enough that they could explain it in plain English to a neighbor. He finds that by his doing so, his patients take better care of their teeth and take ownership of their mouth, thus having fewer problems in the future.

All of these reasons explain why Dr. Faddis doesn't need to advertise or run discount promotions. Nearly all his new patients have been referred to him by his other patients. By building lasting relationships with patients, he has developed a fanatically loyal following. He turns new clients into advocates for his practice who proactively encourage friends and family to go see him. Faddis started out practicing in a crowded dental office for a while.

He was told that dentistry involves getting people numb, treating them, and moving on. The other doctors in the office would each have three chairs going at once, inevitably falling hours behind schedule, turning the treatment room into a small waiting room. The emphasis was on "never letting money walk out the door" if they can be treated today. "It didn't seem right to me," he recalls. The office wasn't putting its patients' interests first, and he was uncomfortable about that. "I thought, this doesn't seem to be working for me." He left the group practice after just six months.

At the time, he was twenty-nine and living in an apartment with his wife, who was expecting their third child. Despite a heavy student loan burden, he started out on his own, very much the underdog, with just one or two patients a week. "I did it the old-fashioned way, just hoping that if I built it they would come," he said. "In doing so, it allowed me to sit with patients. I could spend as much time as needed and never rushed a checkup with anyone, visit with them . . . answer any question they wanted. I thought, you know what? This isn't going to make me a lot of money, but I like it."

Today Faddis practices in surroundings that are deliberately designed not to look or even smell like a dentist's office. The décor is up-to-date, with high-end art on the walls, and the setting is scented in a way to take patients' mind off what they are about to undergo. Sight and smell are important to Faddis, since at most practices, he says, "These two things are very off-putting for dental patients. First impressions of that kind are critical, because by the time I meet a patient, the patient's emotions have already been primed by what they've experienced—the referring source, the act of making the appointment, and the time spent waiting. If all those experiences have been positive, my job is much easier, because my patient is more at ease."

The treatment experience itself is also far removed from the way dentistry is typically practiced. "You walk in, and I'm on time all the time," he says. "We never double or triple book appointments.

We see one patient at a time, and because I'm not running room to room, it's actually more efficient. We have a small staff, focused on one patient, and I do quality work fast, which the patients appreciate. The patient and I are both seated at the same time, and I don't stand up until the treatment is finished. No phone calls, no distractions. Just focused treatment." What's more, he adds, "Patients have been conditioned to think dental treatment and the numbing process take a long time. Wrong! This is a ploy to allow the dentist to leave the first patient and start treatment on a second or third patient. This is inefficient and wastes everyone's time."

Faddis has never hired a hygienist. He does all the teeth-cleaning himself. "That's unheard of in dentistry nowadays," he says. "Dentists don't want to clean teeth. You don't make enough money cleaning teeth to justify doing it. You want to be doing an advanced procedure and not a $100 cleaning. But that's the time to bond with patients. How are you doing? What's going on?" The simplicity of teeth-cleaning gives him time to connect with the patient and gently educate each patient about dental hygiene. It's time he wouldn't have if he delegated cleaning to a hygienist and limited his contact with patients only to the time spent on higher-value procedures.

As a result, he says, "My entire practice is built on word of mouth." By connecting with patients in this way, he hardly ever loses them to other practices, while he continues to get a steady stream of referrals. He doesn't spend any money on advertising and has never needed to. Ultimately, he says, his practice has thrived because he's run it according to the Golden Rule of treating others as he would want to be treated. "I don't like to wait," he says, "so I don't want to see others wait." He takes Fridays off but comes in for emergencies, because that's what he'd want. And he doesn't charge extra for dealing with emergencies. Instead, he's taken care of his customers, and they have responded by becoming his advocates, his evangelists. That's how they return the favor and take care of him.

It wasn't Faddis's intent to become the Mercedes Benz of dentistry, but that's essentially what he's done. Mercedes is a luxury brand, but that's not what sets it apart from other carmakers in terms of customer loyalty. At 55 percent, Mercedes has the highest rate of customer loyalty among all luxury carmakers, so the company attempts to go one better and make customer referrals a business objective.

"Our goal is turn our customers into advocates," says Steve Cannon, president and CEO of Mercedes-Benz USA. "Having a trouble-free, great experience is not enough to turn loyalty into advocacy. If they've had a great experience, that's wonderful, but when we layer on top of that something that truly makes the ownership experience a little more special, a little bit more emotional, then we sort of jump over that hurdle."

For instance, Mercedes practices what it calls "random acts of kindness" with its customers, offering them invitations to exclusive events related to the Masters golf tournament, Fashion Week in New York, or the U.S. Tennis Open. Mercedes's alliance with fourteen exclusive hotels around the country means that when Mercedes drivers check in, they're rewarded with a bottle of wine and a $100 spa and resort credit, presented as tokens of gratitude for Mercedes ownership. Each new buyer of a high-performance AMG Mercedes vehicle gets to schedule a day on a racetrack with a professional driver to learn how to drive the car under extreme, intense conditions.

"The driving experience turns loyalists into—not even advocates—let's call them zealots," Cannon says. "One customer brought his Dad and then he wrote me a letter that said, 'I had the best day with my father that we've ever had in my entire lifetime' . . . That kind of emotion associated with an experience that Mercedes-Benz provided is hard to measure, but it's what turns those people into advocates and zealots."

Steve Cannon is the first to acknowledge that in terms of product quality, all the luxury brands are running very close to each other. "Everyone is getting better at their game," he says. "Quality levels are converging . . . In the car space, nobody needs to drive a $100,000 car, and $20,000 cars keep getting better. So it really boils down to experience . . . to justify a purchase at that level." That puts special pressure on Mercedes dealerships to distinguish themselves, not only from other brands but also from each other. Many Mercedes dealers have welcoming programs for new owners, sending them flowers, birthday cards, and anniversary cards. Cannon points to a southern California dealership that offers free wash-and-vacuum service for the life of the car.

At one such dealership in the Chicago area, Loeber Motors, senior sales manager Bob Dekoy says the entire dealership runs by the founder's credo that "if you don't satisfy the customer, someone else will." He adds, "Basically what I've done is listen to the customer, see what their needs are, and stay in touch with them."[19] He estimates that 60 to 70 percent of sales are from repeat customers, and some customers, he knows, come to Loeber from miles away, driving past other Mercedes dealers in order to give him and Loeber their loyal patronage.

Dekoy says he always assumes that the average Mercedes buyer is smarter than him, and that includes visitors to the dealership who don't look like what might be considered stereotypical Mercedes buyers. He recalls chatting about his cars with a teenager for about half an hour one day, knowing that the young man was probably too young to drive the car, much less buy one. Six months later, the young man returned with his uncle and pointed to Bob as the salesman who had taken such good care of him. The uncle closed on a car that day.

On another occasion, Dekoy saw a young man in his early twenties who was eyeing the most expensive car on the floor. "This guy did not fit the profile of being a Mercedes customer," he recalls. "Nobody even walked up to him, even to see if he wanted a job as a floor sweeper." The young man told Dekoy that he wanted to buy the car, but for the time being all he needed was a brochure. The dealership was out of brochures on that model, but Dekoy offered to take down the young man's name and number. He recognized the last name as belonging to a prominent Chicago family. "The next morning I get a phone call at 9:30," Dekoy says with a laugh. It was the young man's father. "[He said] 'Okay, you've got a blue car in front of your desk, my son wants to buy it, and we'll be in at one o'clock to pick it up.' . . . In addition to that, I've probably sold a dozen cars to that family since then, and I'm still selling them cars now."

Kelly Faddis and Bob Dekoy succeed by passing the loyalty tests of their customers—loyalty tests that their competitors often fail. For loyal customers to trust, commit, and support them, each of those businesses first had to demonstrate genuine warmth, concern, and commitment to those customers' needs and interests. As you'll see, customers handsomely reward companies and brands that exercise this simple but powerful application of warmth and competence insights, through something called the *principle of worthy intentions*. When a company or brand goes above and beyond normal expectations to express worthy intentions, it turns loyal customers into passionate advocates who actively recommend others to them.

Chapter Three

The Principle of Worthy Intentions

The simple and reliable way to demonstrate warmth and competence

Carolyn Beauchesne says she's an addict, but that she's got her problem under control. Back in 2008, the mother of three from Orange County, California, decided to reward herself for hitting her weight-loss goal at the gym by buying some new workout clothes from Lululemon, the trendsetting clothing store that had recently opened in Newport Beach.

In the following five years, Beauchesne estimates she spent about $25,000 at Lululemon. She knows because she keeps a spreadsheet record of all her purchases. Her blog, "Lululemon Addict," attracts sixty-five thousand unique visitors per month, including other loyal "Lulu-heads," as they're sometimes called, who send her photos of themselves in the store's latest creations. Her blog includes a glossary of insider terms for "Lulu newbies" including this one: "Angel—someone who will go to one of their local stores and buy lulu for you (since your store doesn't have it or you don't live near one) and mail it to you." What other retailer has its customers running shopping errands for each other out of sheer mutual love of its products?

Lululemon has taken the women's activewear industry by storm. Started in 2000 in Vancouver, Canada, as a single yoga gear store, it has expanded rapidly to more than two hundred stores in North America and Australia. Despite high prices for products that often sell out fast, the retailer has developed an almost cultlike following among its loyal fans. Beauchesne explained to *Business Insider* in 2012, "Their clothes really fit me and the fabric is higher-quality than other brands." She added that they appeal in particular to older women: "You aren't forced to work out with a big 'PINK' written on your butt, their clothes aren't so sexy or revealing that you feel self-conscious."[1]

Despite a brief period of yoga pants recalls in early 2013, fans of Lululemon are clearly sold on the company's *competence*, on the quality and fit of its unique products. They love the way Lululemon fabrics and designs flatter their figures and swear by its reputation for holding up under repeated washings, with trademarked performance materials such as "Luon" and "silverescent," which includes odor-reducing silver fibers. Yoga pants, which can be gotten on sale for under $50 at competing retailers, start at $78 at Lululemon, and they are almost never available at a discount. Lulu fans think the products are worth the cost, because almost 95 percent of all Lululemon purchases are made at full price.

There are a good number of unique ways, however, in which Lululemon draws in its fans with *warmth* as well as competence. Lululemon stores tend to be small and are left a little messy on purpose, to project a relaxed, lived-in look. Pants are hemmed for free.[2] Customers are called "guests." Sales clerks are called "eds," for educators, and they are better trained and better paid than most other retail clerks, and they're expected to educate customers about the clothing and help them find the perfect fit. (Even the clothing tags are educational, with each one carrying a message of "Why we made this.")

But the real difference in Lululemon is the way that each individual store builds a community around itself. As far in advance as a year before each new store is set to open, Lululemon scouts the immediate area to identify influential local yoga and fitness instructors who would be willing to become Lululemon's "community ambassadors." The ambassadors get discounts on Lululemon clothing, and in exchange their classes are promoted by Lululemon online and inside the stores. Lululemon ambassadors also lead free running clubs and yoga classes. The yoga sessions are often held right on the floors of the stores themselves, before the store opens, with the open racks shoved to the sides.

The company's vision statement, prominently displayed in every store, reflects founder Chip Wilson's stated desire "to elevate the world from mediocrity to greatness." The guiding philosophy of the company is reflected in inspiring phrases imprinted on its sales bags ("Do one thing a day that scares you"). Lululemon's culture encourages its guests to set goals for themselves, and not just fitness goals, either. The website offers a free downloadable goal-setting worksheet to help you "create your ideal life."

Lululemon communicates a message that the store is a place that supports your pursuit of yoga, and of your ideal life, whether you buy something there or not. In so many ways, the company expends time and resources putting the customer's interests ahead of its own, and the response has been overwhelming. On a revenue-per-square-foot basis, Lululemon in 2012 ranked third behind only Apple and Tiffany & Co.[3] Buoyed by the fanatical loyalty of its guests, Lululemon has emerged from nowhere to become one of the most profitable clothing stores on earth.

Wall Street doesn't really understand how Lululemon generates its extraordinary loyalty. Analysts in earnings calls ask if Lululemon has done formal research on how the brand is viewed (Lululemon hasn't and refuses to), and they question such practices as deliberately limiting stocks of popular products. In December 2012, one analyst asked CEO Christine Day why a newly opened store on the Upper West Side of Manhattan didn't even have the company's name on it. Day explained, "We don't believe in putting twelve signs on our store. We're very respectful of being part of the community in the street. And we use community to engage and drive traffic, not signage." Day's point was that if your long-term goal is to build a community around a store, then you want to open up in a respectful way that arouses curiosity and makes Lulu-heads feel special, not with a grand opening that boasts of your presence.

Trust as Our Default

Lululemon's winning formula reflects something we call the *principle of worthy intentions*. This principle is a relationship-building strategy that involves attracting and keeping customers by consistently putting their best interests ahead of those of the company or brand. Some discover this principle out of necessity, but Lululemon is different. The company was founded on this principle and manages by it to this day. Thanks to its exceptional level of warmth and competence, Lululemon is able to maintain a direct dialogue with its customers through its each of its local stores. That one-on-one dialogue is a stark departure from traditional one-way marketing messages because it allows Lululemon to communicate the company's worthy intentions thoroughly to each of its customers.

Businesses face a difficult challenge if they try to gain our loyalty with competence alone. Most of us, most of the time, are perfectly satisfied with the competent goods and services we're already in the habit of buying. We're unlikely to change these habits on rational grounds, especially because differences in comparative quality have become harder and harder to discern. Only the emotional connections of worthy intentions have the power to change minds. When we are offered someone's worthy intentions, in the form of a relationship set openly in our favor, only then are we likely to shift our perspective and try something new.

Chris's colleague Ed Wallace introduced him to the idea that "worthy intent" is the basis for all successful one-on-one customer relationships. Ed describes worthy intent as "the inherent promise you make to keep the other person's best interests at the core of your business relationship."[4]

As Ed sees it, anyone working with customers must express worthy intentions toward their goals, passions, and struggles. It's the only way to advance the relationship and build precious relational capital in an increasingly transactional business environment. Worthy intent, he says, is the "golden rule for client-facing professionals." You must also be credible and competent, of course, but unless you communicate your worthy intent, your clients will always to be tempted to wander off and find others who offer services just as competent, and at a lower cost. In most cases, this involves little things that are relatively easy and inexpensive to offer but send a strong message to customers about the intentions of the seller.

In the Relationship Renaissance, the most valuable commercial relationships take on the character of the traditional one-to-one business relationship. Most companies however, struggle with this paradigm. The previous chapter discussed how companies eagerly roll out costly "loyalty programs" that compensate return customers. Lululemon has perhaps the most loyal customers in retail today, and Lululemon has no loyalty or "rewards" program at all. In fact, Lululemon doesn't even keep data on its individual customers. It spends no money at all on the customer relationship management software (known as CRM) that many retailers rely on to send out little birthday cards, teasers, and discounts to their most loyal customers.

Why? Because Lululemon operates in ways that ensure that its most loyal customers don't need automated acknowledgments via email or the postal service. Loyal "Lulu-heads" get all the real live acknowledgment they can handle at their local stores. Super-loyal "addicts" like Carolyn Beauchesne are known well by the

Lululemon people most important to her—the manager and the eds at her Lululemon location in Newport Beach. Meanwhile, all the resources Lululemon saves by not managing a customer loyalty program can be diverted toward product development (enhancing competence), building community with complimentary yoga classes and local charitable giving (demonstrating warmth), and, of course, profits. Lululemon saves millions by having no national or local advertising budgets at all. In fact, the highest-ranking member of Lululemon's marketing department is the company's "director of community relations."

Lululemon and Honest Tea (previously mentioned in the introduction) are just a few examples of relatively young companies that have grown rapidly without the benefit of mass advertising budgets. They are truly Relationship Renaissance companies, and they illustrate how reliably worthy intentions work with the natural flow of human nature. Worthy intentions invite us to form the trusting relationships that we, as human beings, are primed to prefer. Trust is an efficient and effective form of social intelligence.[5] People who are trusting tend to be more socially successful. They are less suspicious and less lonely. They are also less likely to express feelings of vengefulness and resentment.[6] In economic life, trust enables cooperation for mutual benefit.[7]

Studies show we are much more predisposed to trust other people than we even realize. Our general predilection is to expect good things from most people (unless and until proven otherwise).[8] This predisposition has long been a necessary force to help us adapt to new and unexpected circumstances. Trust requires us to assume that the social world is generally benevolent, having "confidence or faith that some other, upon whom we must depend, will not act in ways that occasion us painful consequences."[9] Although trust makes us vulnerable, it also offers opportunities that more than compensate for the risk.

So when we enter a Lululemon store where the people and the surroundings encourage us to find a perfect-fitting garment (and also encourage us to keep to our personal goals for fitness and even for our ideal life), we are inclined to believe that this is a place worthy of our trust and loyalty, based on its worthy intentions. Our default orientation—to respond to worthy intentions with trust and loyalty—represents a particular opportunity for those companies and brands that, like Lululemon, secure the lasting loyalty and admiration of their customers.

Loyalty as a Primal Attachment

In some important respects, Lululemon falls short of being a shopper's paradise. For one thing, its return policy is highly restrictive. Two weeks is the time limit on returns, and no garment that's been washed or had its price tag removed is accepted for return. The company's CEO has even been quoted as saying about returns, somewhat combatively, "We're not Nordstrom's. We're not your personal shopper."[10]

Lululemon also limits supplies of its high-demand items, which helps breed a must-have-it sensibility among Lulu-heads. They gladly pay the full price today for a garment that may be gone forever tomorrow.[11] By regularly releasing new colors and patterns and then discontinuing them as soon as they sell out, Lululemon also motivates its many loyal customers to keep coming back to the stores regularly, for fear of missing out.

Brain studies investigating the nature of "conditional" and "unconditional" trust may help shed light on why Lululemon fans don't seem to act rationally, nor is there any evidence they take offense at the lack of discounts and the stingy return policies. A team of researchers based at the National Institutes of Health discovered through brain scanning imagery that when we deal with a partner whom we assume is self-interested (as in most commercial transactions), we behave with cautious, conditional trust. Conditional trust activates a higher, more evolved region of the brain, one associated with evaluation of "expected and realized reward"[12]—cost/benefit analysis. Essentially, our brains need to work harder and analyze more data when we are in a situation involving conditional trust. That's why buying a car, or any other high-pressure sales situation, is so stressful for so many people.

On the other hand, when we assume our partner is trustworthy (possessing worthy intentions toward us), we behave with unconditional trust in a way that activates a more primitive part of our brains. This area, which doesn't require our brains to work nearly so hard, is the region of the brain linked to "social attachment behavior."[13] Basically, it's much more pleasurable to behave with unconditional trust, because it's not so taxing, it's not as analytical, and it stimulates the same area of the brain that is stimulated by friends and family. When Lulu-heads say they "love" Lululemon, they really do. They enter the store in a mental state of unconditional trust, prompted by Lululemon's worthy intentions. They feel as though they are among friends and family, and they act accordingly. The $78 yoga pants fly off the racks, without the Lulu-heads overthinking their purchases.

Unconditional trust, however, bears a greater burden than conditional trust. A person in a state of conditional trust is poised to be betrayed and isn't entirely shocked when it happens. Not so with someone possessing unconditional trust. When Lululemon issued an announcement in early 2013 that its popular Luon yoga pants had to be recalled because of customer complaints that the fabric had a sheer see-through quality, the backlash against Lululemon was swift and harsh. Company officials tried in vain to dispel media reports that customers had been forced to prove the faultiness of their yoga pants by submitting to a humiliating bend-over test in the stores. Lululemon's head of products resigned and the shortage of yoga pants was projected to put a $60 million dent in revenues. By June 2013, however, redesigned yoga pants had reached store shelves and Lululemon stock had climbed beyond its price level prior to the recall.[14] Nonetheless, CEO Christine

Day announced that month that she planned to step down as soon as the board had identified her replacement.[15]

"Lululemon used to be known for real bullet-proof quality," Carolyn Beauchesne the Lulu Addict says. "Now the fabric is getting thinner and thinner, the stitching is coming undone. If you read the reviews on the Lululemon.com website, you'll see people writing 'Oh, my things unraveled,' 'This whole seam popped while I was doing a split in class.' Just awful." Beauchesne said she'd noticed the sheer fabric problem more than a year before Lululemon acknowledged it. She says that Lululemon needs to start listening better, and, in terms of quality, to get back to its roots.

Crises like this one often give companies a chance to do just that, as we will explore in Chapter Six. But Lululemon, having gone public in 2007 and replaced its founder as CEO in 2008, wouldn't be the first company to trade on its high reputation for warmth and competence by cutting corners in the name of higher profits. It would be a shame to see Lululemon, a brand built upon worthy intentions toward its customers, squander its reputation for such an unworthy objective.

One-Way Streets

The year 2012 was a good one for the University of Dayton (UD). The school is recognized as one of the top ten Catholic research institutions in the nation, but it faces increasing competition in Ohio and across the country for a dwindling pool of high school graduates. Yet, in 2012, UD made a major improvement in admissions selectivity—a key factor in national rankings—by reducing its acceptance rate to 55 percent, down from 76 percent in the previous year. The school exceeded its freshman enrollment goal by two hundred, even though it had offered admission to one thousand fewer applicants than in 2011.

The one nagging problem in UD's overall picture, though, was its faltering level of alumni giving. The depressed economy had been a contributing factor, no doubt, but the trends were troubling nonetheless. Annual giving to UD had dropped steadily in preceding years and so had the overall percentage of alumni who had given. As with nearly all universities, UD relied heavily on telephone fundraising for a significant portion of its outreach to alumni, and results were flagging from that activity in particular.

After UD hired Chris to evaluate the university's relationships with its alumni, he and his team interviewed nearly four thousand alumni to assess their warmth and competence perceptions of UD, as well as their loyalty to the institution. If the down economy were truly the source of the problem with their fundraising efforts, the results would show that although UD alumni feel strong loyalty to the school, they are simply unable to contribute during tough times.

However, that's not what the results showed at all. Rather, the alumni perceptions of UD's warmth and competence were the most important determinants of their loyalty to the school. What's more, UD's warmth, competence, and loyalty ratings explained nearly half of all the actual giving behavior that these four thousand alumni had engaged in over the past twenty years. In fact, the 29 percent of the alumni who were most proud, enthusiastic, and loyal to UD were contributing more than half of all alumni gifts. The other 71 percent of alumni varied greatly in their feelings toward the school and in their financial contributions.

The most striking revelation, though, was that the alumni who contribute the most financially to UD were not necessarily the ones with the greatest wealth. Some alumni with the least financial means ranked among the highest and most frequent donors, while others, who reported giving substantial sums of money to other charities, were giving little or nothing to their alma mater.

What did UD's top donors have in common? They were those who most strongly perceived Dayton as warm and competent. Top donors were much more likely than others to agree with statements such as "UD communicates clearly and effectively," "UD listens well and is responsive to my needs," "UD always acts with my best interests in mind," "UD helps me accomplish my goals," and "UD offers high quality advice and assistance."

Chris's analytics team conducted some heavy number crunching and developed a structural equation model that documented the relationships among warmth, competence, loyalty, and alumni giving. The analysis revealed that for every one-point increase in perceived warmth on a seven-point scale, overall loyalty to UD would increase by .41 points. In addition, for every one-point increase in overall loyalty to UD, the average annual gift would increase 23 percent, adding over $60 for each alumnus every year.

Among those who rated UD lower on warmth and competence, the study discovered an unpleasant fact. UD's aggressive telephone fundraising was doing something much worse than missing its dollar goals. It was actually communicating unworthy intentions and alienating over half the alumni population. Alumni comments included statements such as "The only time I hear from UD is when they want money," "100 percent fed up with the phone calls asking for a donation," and "I find your requests for 'charitable donations' to be insulting and disgusting."

When Chris shared his findings with university officials, his first and most urgent recommendation was that the telephone fundraising be curtailed dramatically. His longer-term

Figure 3.1. Impact of Warmth, Competence, and Loyalty on Annual Giving to UD

recommendation was that fundraising efforts at UD shouldn't begin and end with appeals for money. Any fundraising strategy should begin with efforts to nurture warmer and more competent relationships with alumni, so that those relationships foster among alumni deeper feelings of loyalty to the school. By focusing first on fulfilling the warmth and competence expectations of alumni, UD will greatly strengthen the loyalty they feel toward the university. As the financial analysis clearly shows, this in turn stimulates more voluntary annual gifts from more alumni seeking to reciprocate the worthy intentions they've been shown by UD.

Within the university administration, Chris's study has been embraced as an opportunity for UD to become a genuine innovator in the field of alumni development and university advancement, just as they have in the field of student enrollment. "This work has enabled us to achieve a paradigm shift in our core activities," said David Harper, UD's vice-president for university advancement. "The old paradigm was about fundraising. Now it's about relationship management, of which fundraising is just one of the outcomes." UD has begun to evaluate the university's relationships with all its stakeholders—students, faculty, staff, and even applicants—along the same lines of warmth, competence, and loyalty. Sundar Kumarasamy, UD's vice president for enrollment and marketing, is so taken with the approach that he predicts it "will define the future of this industry, and in ten years will likely become the standard."

When Chris was growing up, his mother would sometimes admonish her children for selfish or self-centered behavior by saying, "You know, they name *streets* after people like you. They're called '*one way streets*'!"

"One-way" thinking can overtake any organization that makes a priority of short-term financial results at the expense of human relationships. When the University of Dayton's development office stepped up the pace of its gift requests in an effort to bolster its flagging fundraising results, there was probably little thought given to the effect of making hundreds of alumni phones ring off their hooks. The message, though, was loud and clear: "You only want me for my money, and now you won't stop pestering me."

UD is now working to counteract this perception with an outreach program based on worthy intentions. The new goal is to rebuild and strengthen alumni relationships first, by providing support where alumni say they would appreciate it most. The secondary goal is to ask alumni for their support, but only where and when it is welcome. During the 2012–2013 academic year, UD scaled back its fundraising requests dramatically, but saw a 13-percent increase in alumni annual giving revenue, along with a 9-percent jump in the proportion of alumni making gifts that year.

One of the most interesting findings to come out of the UD study was the way the most loyal donors perceived their connections to the university. Overwhelmingly, UD's most consistent donors were those who reported being in close touch with members of their graduating classes. Top donors were also much more likely to have other UD alumni as friends and as members of their professional networks. Alumni who feel that their affiliation with UD is relevant in their daily lives—even in the absence of direct contact with the university—are much more likely to make donations.

Why is that so? Likely it's because their pleasant feelings of social attachment to the university stimulate those same primitive and more trusting areas of the brain discussed earlier in this chapter. With multiple connections to UD, they're not likely to open a fundraising letter with an analytical appraisal of "What's UD done for me lately?" Rather, UD plays an active role in their lives. These alumni give to UD because it feels like their support is staying in the family.

Not unlike the Lululemon store down the block, the UD alumni development office has begun to place its first focus on truly developing a community. The university's expressions of worthy intentions will assure each alumnus that UD would like to be his or her educational partner for life. The office will take on the role of connecting alumni all over the world by offering them local events, continuing education, support, and resources. Any measure that UD takes to build relationships among UD people registers among alumni as a strong demonstration of worthy intentions.

If UD's alumni development office is able to follow through effectively on these plans, consider for a moment what it might accomplish. Sponsoring a series of new support programs and services for alumni would help provide the university with a warmer image, and it would likely also enhance perceptions of the school's competence. This is not to suggest that warmth is just another type of competence. But when any organization consciously pursues a course of worthy intentions, warmth and competence will tend to play off each other. By making the breakthrough of leading with worthy intentions and increasing their perceptions of warmth, they open up new opportunities for developing and expressing competence, too.

To return to Lululemon, there are at least two distinctive practices at their stores that illustrate this point. First, each store features a marker board so customers can leave comments. It is a simple gesture of worthy intentions. Customers feel invited to express themselves, the comments are fun to read, and it adds to the casual, homey store environment. What customers may not know, however, is that these boards also serve a practical function in the running of the company. Comments are collected and sent back to Lululemon's headquarters, a place where they shun formal market research. The boards are another way in which headquarters stays in touch with what Lululemon customers are thinking and saying.

Lululemon employees are also trained to listen closely to customers and even to eavesdrop on them while they're in the changing rooms. The stores are designed with folding tables near the changing rooms so that employees can casually linger and hear customer comments as they try on the clothes. Lululemon wants customers to feel heard, even when they're too polite to complain. Overhearing little grumbles (and inquiring about them tactfully later) ensures that customers are truly satisfied. The practice also functions as a contributor to Lululemon's competence. Store managers become aware of subtle clothing design issues that might require fixing back at headquarters. Close, careful listening of this kind is not just an expression of worthy intentions. It provides Lululemon's design staff with a valuable source of feedback, too.

In both of these cases, warmth brings Lululemon closer to customers, and that closeness makes Lululemon a better, more competent retailer. Warmth can fuel competence. It can inspire the pursuit of new areas of competence, just as it did at the University of Dayton's alumni development office. If you are any good at what you do, expressing your warmth through worthy intentions will open up avenues of opportunity that can make you even better.

Shared Moral Values

A visit to Starbucks headquarters in 2006, while Chris was leading marketing at ARAMARK, was the first time he realized that Starbucks' tremendous success was largely due to something other than the quality of its coffee. At the time, ARAMARK was a licensee of Starbucks and operated about forty of its coffee shops on college campuses. But ARAMARK had been struggling to deliver the kind of customer experience that Starbucks was known for. So a team of executives was dispatched to spend a few days in Seattle to learn more about the company's operational philosophy and approach. During the visit, Chris was given a copy of Starbucks' *Green Apron Book*, a little employee handbook sized to fit inside the pocket of a Starbucks apron.

The book describes for employees what Starbucks calls "The Five Ways of Being," which are: be welcoming, be genuine, be considerate, be knowledgeable, be involved. For each of these ways of being, the book offers specific examples of behaviors that describe what that way of being looks like. For "be welcoming," Starbucks emphasizes the importance of welcoming people by name if they're regulars. When you order a drink at Starbucks, they write your name on the paper cup, and then when your order is ready, your name is called out. That's a part of feeling welcomed at Starbucks. You are known for your name, you're not known as "venti mocha latte."

Perhaps most surprising, these "Ways of Being" weren't just training ideas that sat on a shelf somewhere. They were the core management approach in every location. Managers were expected to practice these same principles in supporting their "associates" and actively recognize them when they did the same with customers. During the Starbucks immersion visit, Chris and the rest of the group were told story after story of how employees and managers were living these principles with customers every day.

In one particularly memorable story, they were told about a Starbucks store where a quiet, elderly man named Pete came in every morning for a simple cup of coffee. The Starbucks baristas greeted him by name, and they would say goodbye if they noticed him leaving. Pete had been a regular at the store for a few years, and then his visits suddenly stopped.

Some weeks later, a young woman showed up at the store asking if anyone there knew of an older man named Pete, and of course, everyone did. She told the employees that Pete was her father, and that he had recently passed away. While cleaning out her father's apartment, the young woman had come across a large plastic bag filled with empty Starbucks cups that Pete evidently couldn't bear to throw out. Each one was marked with a handwritten "Pete," accompanied by a little smiley face. The young woman said she felt she had to stop by and thank the Starbucks employees for being so kind to her father. Although he had never mentioned it to his family, his daily visits there had apparently meant a lot to him.

Starbucks employees and managers pass along stories of this kind all the time, presumably to impress upon a mostly younger workforce that no one can ever really know the effect they might be having on their customers. A lot of people go to Starbucks because Starbucks is competent at making good coffee consistently and reliably. For those customers, the warmth that Starbucks delivers through its pleasant staff and store environment is enjoyed as a bonus.

But for some customers, like that elderly gentleman Pete, Starbucks' warmth might be considered its most important area of competence. Social psychology tells us that belonging is one of our essential human needs.[16] For Pete, that vital sense of belonging was found each morning with his ritual visit to Starbucks.

If you look at Starbucks' five ways of being again, consider that three of them—welcoming, considerate, and genuine,—describe widely accepted warm, moral, and ethical modes of behavior. It may cost Starbucks more to hire, manage, and retain only those employees who can represent the company consistently with such behavior, but the sum effect is largely what inspires our loyalty to Starbucks.

For thousands of years, we have defined our tribes by those who share our moral values. The companies toward which we feel true relational loyalty prompt us, with their benevolent gestures, to think of them differently in a *literal* sense, by stirring the region of the human brain reserved for easy interactions with friends and family. When organizations such as Lululemon, Starbucks, or the University of Dayton manage to offer us the experience of their selfless worthy intentions, our minds react unconsciously in ways that have little to do with commerce and dollars and everything to do with our hard-wired need for tribal belonging.

Doing Well by Doing Good

Back in the early 1990s, Connecticut bike shop owner Chris Zane wrestled with a problem that had stumped bike shop owners all over the country: how to compete with Wal-Mart. Especially in the children's bike market, Wal-Mart and other mass retailers are able to import extremely inexpensive bikes with 12-inch wheels and put them on sale for as little as $69. For most bicycle retailers, who carry only higher-end, higher-quality bicycles, that price is untouchable. Chris Zane faced the question of how to market $129 children's bicycles that he knew were more durable and would provide children and their parents with a better experience.

In *Reinventing the Wheel*, Zane describes how he decided that there was much more than a $129 sale at stake in the way he approached this problem. In a discussion with his store manager, he observed that parents are apt to take the cheaper route with a child's bike because children outgrow bicycles so fast. The store manager responded with the suggestion that Zane's Cycles should make a promise to each buyer of a child's bike: When your child outgrows it, bring it back, and you can trade it in for a full-price credit toward a bigger bike. The $129 price for that 12-inch bike could be applied to toward the $329 price of a 16-inch bike, and then that bike might be traded in years later for full credit toward a more expensive 26-inch bike.

"I have to admit," Zane wrote, "that when Tom first told me about the program, I started to sweat a little. All I could see were rows and rows filled with thousands of returned children's bikes we'd be stuck with."[17] But Tom, the store manager, reminded his boss that the trade-in offer is a way of generating relational loyalty among the parents. This simple expression of worthy intentions would likely establish relationships with customers that might last for decades.

After several seasons under the trade-in policy, Zane noticed a funny thing. Only about 20 percent of the children's bicycles he sold were coming back for trade-ins. His first concern had been that the program might work too well. Now he was worried that it wasn't working at all. So he began calling up customers to remind them that if their children were outgrowing their bikes, it might be time to return for an upgrade.

What Zane discovered in those calls was that most people didn't want to trade in their children's bikes. Because the bikes were higher quality than the ones sold at Wal-Mart, they were holding up exceptionally well under their children's rough handling and abuse. Most parents were so attached to the bikes that they preferred to pass them on to friends and relatives with younger children. Zane points out, "When we started looking at the program in this light, we realized that not only had we boosted our sales, without discounting them, for our kids' bikes, we also helped our customers recognize the quality of our bikes."

Zane estimates that the lifetime value of each of his customers is $12,500 in revenue, of which $5,600 is profit. With that much money at stake, his shop offers customers an absolute guarantee of satisfaction. He will take back any bicycle for full price if the customer isn't satisfied, even if, as it was in one case, the bicycle is five years old. He also offers lifetime service on every bicycle he sells in the form of free tune-ups and repairs for everyday wear and tear. When he instituted that program in 1995, national bicycle trade journals ran letters calling him crazy for giving away services for free. Instead, he drove his competitors crazy—and drove some of them out of business.

Chris Zane has since become something of a prophet for the principle of worthy intentions among the nation's small retailers. He books speaking engagements in which he advocates for the absolute necessity of store owners' maintaining relational loyalty as the number one objective in everything they do. Competing on price against the likes of Wal-Mart and Target is useless, so worthy intentions become their primary competitive edge.

Zane uses this simple example of one way he's built a sense of trust with his customers: every bike part that costs him less than a dollar is given away free. He used to charge about $1.99 for tiny little parts that cost him nearly nothing—nuts, bolts, ball bearings, and the small master links on the bicycle's drive chain. But then he realized that the need for these parts "come during painful times for our customers." A father who enters Zane's with a crying child and a bike with a broken chain has enough troubles without being nickel-and-dimed for a master link. So Zane started giving away the parts for free.

"We do this because it lets our customers know we're not out to milk them," he writes. "We're there to save them the hassle and the expense of getting their kids back out on the street and riding their bikes."[18] When he tracked the annual expense of these little giveaways, he discovered it had cost him just $86 to offer free parts to 450 customers—which represented 450 chances to make a lasting impression and show worthy intentions toward customers with whom he expects a lifelong relationship.

Deserving and Undeserving Success

Zane's Cycles registers as a business with worthy intentions only if we perceive his shop as both warm *and* competent. An incompetent bike shop that gives away free stuff and offers guaranteed satisfaction would more likely foster feelings of pity and indifference, but not loyalty. The worthy intentions expressed through so many of Chris Zane's practices enhance his shop's reputation, even among those who don't trade in their children's bikes and never take advantage of the offer to return unsatisfactory products. Zane, in that sense, is generally seen as *deserving* his success, and that's important to how people judge him. Perceptions of competent people and companies that lack warmth provoke feelings of envy and grudging cooperation. In a similar vein, people judge other people's success by whether they deserve it, not just by whether they've earned it. Deservingness therefore has elements of both perceived competence (earned) but also perceived warmth (deserved).

Studies show that reactions to other people's successes or failures depend on whether their outcomes seem to be deserved.[19] If someone succeeds through a system of values that is alien to us (a slumlord, perhaps, or the owner of an overpriced convenience store), we're ready to acknowledge that the success is *earned*, but less likely to feel warmth toward the individual as someone *deserving* our admiration and loyalty. A convenience store with high prices does not win our loyalty. It gets only our regular business and our grudging compliance.

On the other hand, Zane's Cycles, much like Lululemon and Starbucks, also charges comparatively high prices. These businesses don't need to rely on discounts and promotions as their competitors do, because the relationship-based loyalty they enjoy with customers lowers their costs and provides them with more predictable revenues. In Zane's case, our sense of his *deservingness*, inspired by all of his worthy intentions, overcomes whatever objections we might have to his prices. The free service, the free little parts, and the lifetime guarantees all make us feel like Zane's reflects our moral values, our sense of deservingness, and all the other things that lead us to respect, admire, and want to be a part of those who rank high in warmth and competence.[20]

A handful of national retailers, such as L.L. Bean and Orvis sporting goods, also cultivate their reputation for deservingness by offering lifetime guarantees for everything they sell. Yes, these policies are prone to some occasional abuse: Orvis, for instance, has been known to refund the cost of twenty-year-old tents that have ripped. But officials at both companies say that the policies are well worth risk in the goodwill they earn. They even promote the occasional incidents of customers' abuse of the policies as a way of proving how dedicated they are to taking seriously every customer's claim to satisfaction.

Chobani yogurt is emerging on the scene as an example of how worthy intentions can cultivate feelings of shared moral and cultural values—even when the charismatic founder of the company shares very few outwardly American cultural attributes. Hamdi Ulukaya is a Turkish-born ethnic Kurd who in 2005 was operating a feta cheese plant in New York as an arm of his family's dairy business in Turkey. That year he purchased an old Kraft yogurt plant with the goal of creating a European-style high-protein strained yogurt (commonly known as Greek yogurt to U.S. shoppers). Ulukaya loved America, but he hated its commercially available yogurt. For eighteen months he worked with a Turkish yogurt master to come up with the perfect recipe for a strained yogurt that, in 2007, would be launched as Chobani, or "shepherd" in Turkish.

During those days, the locals in New Berlin, New York, took pity on Ululaya, as someone who was warm but probably incompetent. The local pizza shop owner didn't even have the heart to charge him for lunch. She told an interviewer, "He would tell us all of these things . . . we would be very supportive, and I knew at leaving I'd be like, 'Oh, my God, I'm going to feel so bad when he goes bankrupt. And he's going to lose his shirt.'"[21]

Instead, Chobani took off. Under the tagline "Nothing but good," to distinguish it from U.S. yogurts containing thickeners and starches, sales of Chobani rocketed from $50 million to $700 million in four short years, during a period when the economy was in recession. As with Lululemon, Chobani's meteoric rise was accomplished without any help from mass media. Ulukaya relied on social media to grow a cult of "Chobaniacs" with hundreds of thousands of followers on Facebook and Twitter. He told one interviewer, "The communication is so fast, you don't need huge money for the marketing for your voice to be heard. It's a flat world."[22]

It's significant that when Chobani finally did make its first national advertising push, the ads put Chobaniacs, not Chobani, in center stage. One spot featured a fan who rode his bike eighty miles just to visit the Chobani plant, and another featured a Virginia accountant who schemed to hide her Chobani in the office fridge to keep it from getting swiped by coworkers.[23] Most communications from Chobani seem to have a way of flattering the customer before proclaiming the yogurt's quality. One humble expression that's found frequently in Chobani corporate statements is "Chobani was founded on the belief that people have great taste; they just need great options."[24]

And "Nothing but good" has since evolved from a clever marketing line to what Chobani regards as its guiding philosophy. The company pledges its support for local dairy farmers and economically struggling upstate New York communities. Unusual for a high-growth startup, Chobani gives 10 percent of its annual profits to charity. The company's charitable arm, the Shepherd's Gift Foundation, has donated $1 million to famine relief efforts in Somalia and has leveraged its social media to support the cause.

With 100 percent ownership of his company, Ulukaya is a newly minted billionaire who, when he speaks, hits all the right notes for the Relationship Renaissance. In interviews he is careful to turn all the credit back to his workers, to the throngs of Chobaniacs, and to his adopted homeland. "We have started four years ago with five people," he told an interviewer in 2011. "Right now in the same place we employ a thousand people. It is not me. It is not the—you know, it is not the yogurt. It's the people. It's the spirit. Everybody really wants to go work hard and get things done. And this is the American way."[25] Ulukaya's praise of his American workers and his invocation of shared American ideals is a good way to frame a Turkish-American success story as an American success story for an American audience. His message of worthy intentions is one that resonates and builds loyalty among customers of all shapes, sizes, and ethnicities. This ability to perceive and judge the intentions and abilities of others has been imprinted on us over thousands of generations. As a result, no new technologies or innovations—not even the Internet—can materially change how it continues to guide us during our lifetime, as the next chapter will show.

Chapter Four

The Price of Progress

How faceless commerce leads to a focus on discounts

In 2011, Groupon.com held the distinction of being the fastest-growing internet company in history. In 2012, it held another distinction—the fastest-falling tech stock since the dot-com bubble. The rise and fall of Groupon's daily e-mails of discounted deals could have been foreseen by anyone familiar with the warmth and competence model. Offering deep discounts does not win you hoards of new, loyal customers, as Groupon claimed, any more than you can buy someone's love. Groupon and its many imitators are to customer loyalty what singles bars are to weddings: sometimes a connection at one may lead to the other, but not very often.

The initial allure of Groupon was unmistakable. Imagine yourself as the owner of a local cafe that's been hammered by the recession. Each afternoon, you are confronted with empty tables and idled wait staff. Then a salesperson from Groupon offers you a free marketing campaign with no money down. You get a free promotion aimed at bringing in new customers; all you have to do is offer a discount of 50 percent or more and then split all your proceeds fifty-fifty with Groupon. Any money you lose in offering the discount, the sales rep explains, will be more than made up in full-priced repeat business from all the new customers you'll attract. You're not sure that's true, but business is down, and you've got to try something.

That was the general attitude of owner Jessie Burke at Posies Bakery and Cafe in Portland, Oregon. In March 2010, Posies offered Groupon members $13 worth of baked goods for just $6, and within a month, the cafe was overwhelmed with customers waving their Groupon discounts. A few of those new Groupon customers have since become regulars at Posies, but most of them merely came and went, while helping spoil Posies' atmosphere for its already-loyal clientele in the process. "[W]e met many, many terrible Groupon customers," Jessie wrote later. These included "customers that didn't follow the Groupon rules and used multiple Groupons for single transactions, and argued with you about it with disgusted looks on their faces, or who tipped based on what they owed (10% of $0 is zero dollars, so tossing in a dime was them being generous)."[1]

When customers arrive at an establishment for the main purpose of getting a bargain, they are entering with less-than-worthy intentions. They are motivated more by the joy of getting one over on the proprietor, at least to some extent. For many of them, the least of their concerns is how that proprietor and the employees judge their behavior.

This "Groupon effect" on customer behavior is no small matter. One study by a Rice University researcher reached the surprising conclusion that the single most important factor in whether a Groupon promotion succeeds was "satisfied employees." The study found that how the employees were affected by the promotion was a more reliable predictor of its profitability than the percentage of discount offered, the number of Groupons sold, or the percentage of Groupon users who returned as full-price customers.

"Because the Groupon customer base is made up of deal-seekers and bargain shoppers, they might not tip as well as an average customer," study author Utpal Dholakia said in an interview. "So employees need to be prepared for this type of customer and the sheer volume of customers that might come through."[2]

Groupon-induced crowding can drive down an establishment's perceived warmth *and* competence. A loyal customer's experience at her favorite café might be shattered by a wait staff stretched too thin, longer lines at the register, and the risk of waiting in line behind someone arguing whether a Groupon discount is valid. One hair salon booked so many Groupon customers at a discount that it found it could no longer schedule convenient appointments for its most loyal and highest-paying customers.[3]

The final straw for Posies was when a longtime loyal customer named Lucinda complained to Jessie Burke about having her Groupon offer declined by the owner because it was one day past the expiration date. Lucinda felt that she deserved better as a longtime supporter, and that the rejection made her feel like she never wanted to come back. So Burke wrote a blog post, which has since made the rounds of the Internet, stating, "in short, dear Lucinda and anyone else that comes in with a Groupon in hand, please know that our respectful decline of your coupon is not personal. It's because we cannot afford to lose any more money on this terrible decision I made, and the only saving grace we had was an expiration date."[4]

The Loyalty Disconnect

For some merchants and businesses, Groupon and its many imitators have been, without a doubt, a godsend in terms of short-term revenue. One early success touted by Groupon was a $25 ticket for a Chicago architectural boat tour that was sold for $12 in 2010. Groupon dealt 19,822 tickets in eight hours and split the $238,000 in revenue with the boat tour company. Without Groupon, that $119,000 cash infusion would have likely been lost to the tour operator in the form of empty seats. But how many of those $12 boat riders are apt to come back at full fare? And how did those hoards of casual Groupon day trippers (who were quite possibly bored by architecture) affect the experience of loyal boat tour customers who had paid full fare?

It's perhaps unfair to single out Groupon for these kinds of problems, because the rise of the Internet has created similar problems in almost every industry. Online purchases of everything, including even college degrees, have made customers so price-focused and lacking in loyalty that merchants have responded with any number of price-dependent gimmicks to win them back. The most common, referenced briefly in Chapter Two, are the reward-based "loyalty" programs, which don't really create relational loyalty at all, but merely drive repeat business, at ever-lower prices. With the help of e-commerce, rewards programs have moved far beyond what they were just a few years ago, when Subway would punch your ticket for a free hoagie after ten purchases. They have grown more sophisticated, more complex, and more costly.

Many industries have begun to head down the same road that the hotel industry took more than fifteen years ago. At first, e-commerce was greeted by the hotel industry as a potential cost-savings bonanza. Since then, as the number of hotel reservations made online has crept up to 70 percent, e-commerce has instead evolved into a grim necessity at best, and a ruinously complex headache at its worst.

Expedia, Orbitz, and Hotels.com, known collectively as OTAs (online travel agencies), have become the tails wagging the dog in the travel industry. When the industry was hit hard following the terror attacks of September 11, 2001, OTAs scooped up unsold rooms from struggling hotel owners and resold them to bargain-hunting travelers. By training us to think in terms of comparative price, location, and basic amenities, e-commerce has tended to obscure the importance of service, staff, and reputation-related differences.

In the following years, hoteliers found themselves heavily dependent on OTAs for reservations, even as they were forced to compete with them in the sale of their rooms. Although the hotel companies eventually developed their own sophisticated websites in an attempt to recapture online sales, the price transparency driven by the OTAs forced them to match OTA prices or risk losing otherwise loyal customers to them.

A digital arms race eventually emerged, in which hoteliers, OTAs, and other online travel resellers have used increasingly sophisticated revenue management systems and teams to constantly monitor and tweak hotel rates, trying to gain an edge and squeeze just a few extra dollars from customers. The hotels' reward-based "loyalty" programs, touched on in Chapter Two, had been one of their few competitive advantages, but now the OTAs are creating their own rewards programs.

So all the convenience, efficiency, and savings offered by e-commerce have greatly diluted whatever trust and loyalty might have existed between hoteliers and their customers. Lost in the process are the warmth-and-competence-filled contact, interactions, and relationships between guests and hoteliers that once resulted in relational customer loyalty. It was once cost-effective to fully staff a hotel with warm and competent employees capable of demonstrating worthy intentions toward the guests because those guests could be counted on to reward such treatment with their loyalty. Now the temptation of bargain prices, gained at the click of a mouse, has placed that model of hotel management in danger of extinction.

Similar changes have been visited on the airline and rental car industries, thanks to e-commerce and the influence of the OTAs. Groupon wants to spread it even further. Deflated by the public's weariness with chasing daily deals, Groupon has launched an incentive program called Groupon Rewards, which the founder once proclaimed would make Groupon the "operating system for local commerce." If it were to gain steam, Groupon Rewards would spread this logic of race-to-the-bottom discounting throughout the economy.

The power of the Internet to drive down prices while commoditizing products and services provides evidence for the idea that there is something inherently inhuman about e-commerce. But that's hardly the case. As we know from studies of the Internet's effects on social life, it is easy to use computer technology to maintain rich friendships that don't differ appreciably from face-to-face relationships. The closest previous technological analogue to the Internet was the telephone. An influential paper published in 2004 noted that the telephone, too, was initially greeted with concerns that it would damage loyal face-to-face relationships between and among friends and family. The effect, of course, has been the opposite. The telephone increased our ability to connect with people we value, even if they live far away, and it has also served to strengthen, rather than weaken, local ties.[5]

The Internet and Its Uses

A handful of companies, some with enviably loyal customers, refuse to use the Internet to play the loyalty and rewards card game. Among them is Publix supermarkets, one of the most beloved grocery chains in the southeast United States. "Publix does not have a loyalty card program because we don't think you should need a card to save money at Publix," a spokesperson for the company once stated. "We value all of our customers and we want them all to have a pleasant shopping experience."[6]

Lululemon, another company that earns high loyalty without loyalty cards, uses the Internet to build relationships, by putting the names and faces of its local brand ambassadors on its websites and encouraging local store managers to maintain their own Facebook pages—an almost unheard-of level of staff autonomy granted by a major corporation.

If a company's website is used for interactive relationships and not for one-way commerce, then it can be a powerful tool for communicating a company's warmth and competence through its expression of worthy intentions. Large corporations cannot love us back, but if company employees can use websites, Facebook, Twitter, or other social media to give us the experience of individuality and responsiveness, then the prospects for relational loyalty are there, even though the communications are transacted online.

A number of academic studies have shown that we interact with both computers and websites as what are called "social actors."[7] We are not delusional. We do not "think" they are human. However, we inherently know that computers and websites were created by people. As a result, we process our experiences of interacting with them as a reflection of the intentions and abilities of those that built them, using the same warmth and competence perceptions that guide our behavior toward people, companies, and brands. But we also respond measurably to both computers and websites with human emotion, as evidenced by our tendency to treat them with that most human of attributes—politeness.

Researchers at the University of North Carolina gave students an online tutoring session through a fictitious website, and then provided them with an online questionnaire to rate the quality of the session for a series of factors such as "accurate," "competent," "friendly," "fair," and "warm." They discovered that the students' judgments were more generous if they answered the questionnaire on the same computer and through the same website that offered them the tutorial, and less generous if the students were told to switch computers and log onto a different website in order to judge the online tutoring session. In other words, they were acting with unconscious politeness toward the tutoring websites and the computers they worked with, as though the websites and computers had feelings that might be hurt by low ratings.

"We found evidence that suggests humans can exhibit politeness toward websites and literally (not virtually) treat them as social actors," the paper states, adding that the construct they used to define the quality of politeness "was found to be closely related to the fundamental constructs people use to rapidly assess their social environment: Warmth and Competence."[8]

The research suggests that our natural human affinity for warmth and competence has also prepared us to approach the digital world in a more personal way when we're afforded the chance. In most cases, however, businesses use the Internet solely to achieve economies of scale; the digital world then becomes complicit in damaging customer loyalty and relationships. The Internet, to that extent, can be used to extend the Middle Ages of Marketing into the current day and to continue the practice of using one-way transactions that alienate companies and brands from customers.

Big Love

In February 2013, Chris conducted a customer loyalty study of six of America's largest retailers and confirmed the extent to which we recognize expressions of worthy intentions and detect warmth and competence through our online shopping experiences (see Figure 4.1). The research involved two online retailers (Amazon and Zappos) and four other retailers that sell through online websites plus brick-and-mortar retail stores (Sears, Wal-Mart, Best Buy, and Macy's). A familiar pattern emerged in the results among the group of the four big, legacy brick-and-mortar retailers. Customers ranked each brand as more competent than warm, just as had been found in Chris and Susan's previous studies. However, in each case the websites of these retailers were given a greater edge of competence over warmth than the physical stores.

This response seems logical. Online stores are impersonal, efficient, and convenient. Physical stores, filled as they are with people, faces, and conversations, offer more opportunities for warmth and worthy intentions to be displayed.

However, the research relating to Zappos suggest that a warmth deficiency is not necessarily an attribute of all online retail sites. Zappos was the only one of the six retailers that customers actually rated slightly higher on warmth than on competence—despite its total lack of physical stores. Zappos proves that it's possible for an online store to demonstrate warmth—the key to our relational customer loyalty—through its policies, practices, and website functionality. Even Amazon, which is noted for its absence of human presence on its site, rated surprisingly high on warmth.

In fact, for both brick-and-mortar and online retailers, customer warmth perceptions were more strongly correlated with loyalty than were competence dimensions. What's more, these same warmth dimensions explained an even greater proportion of online customer loyalty than they did brick-and-mortar loyalty. As a result, it's clear that warmth and worthy intentions are just as important for building customer loyalty online as they are offline.

Further analysis revealed that although many customers had made purchases only from the legacy brick-and-mortar stores, *no one* reported making *only* an online purchase from any of these

Figure 4.1.   Impact of Warmth and Competence Perceptions on Customer Loyalty

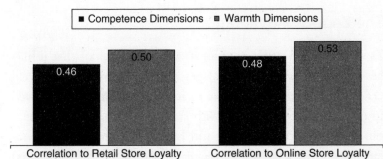

four retailers. Every customer who had made an online purchase at one of these retailers had also made a purchase at its corresponding brick-and-mortar store, presumably beforehand. This behavior pattern suggests that for retailers with both online and physical stores, the success of their online stores is highly dependent on whatever customer loyalty is engendered in their brick-and-mortar stores.

For Best Buy and Sears, this finding poses a serious problem. Both of these big retailers have plans to shutter hundreds of brick-and-mortar stores in the coming years. If their physical stores are gateways to their online stores, then closing down physical stores means that Best Buy and Sears are also closing off channels for customers to get to know them well enough to feel comfortable buying from them online.

And yet, customers who shopped a brand's online site reported much higher loyalty to the brand than those who had never made an online purchase. It seems that for shoppers at brick-and-mortar stores, those experiences play an important role in building loyalty to the point where online purchases can occur. Only those customers who had developed high trust and loyalty with the brick-and-mortar stores felt comfortable enough to begin making purchases online. The problem for these retailers, even the healthier ones such as Wal-Mart and Macy's, is that they have yet to figure out how to make their online stores anything more than adjuncts to their physical stores.

The Zappos Advantage

Zappos has been singled out for so many distinctions that it may be hard to believe that social perception research could reveal yet another one: a rare online store whose warmth is perceived to exceed its competence—with strong ratings in both categories. Zappos' secret, if it can still be called a secret, lies with a customer loyalty team ("customer service" at other companies) that exudes worthy intentions. Zappos, perhaps alone among online retailers, strongly encourages its customers to call, email, or chat directly with its loyalty team—twenty-four hours a day, seven days a week, all year long. The Zappos toll-free customer service number appears at the top of every page of the Zappos website—unheard of in an industry that usually tries to hide help-desk phone numbers and does everything possible to prevent such calls from happening.

The customer loyalty team practices are so indulgent of customer desires that they almost defy bottom-line business sense. The highly trained customer loyalty team members are given a wide degree of latitude in delivering on Zappos' number one cultural imperative: "Deliver the wow experience." A team member named Shaea Labus made this report, released to *Business Insider*, "On July 16th I received a call from Lisa about 2 hrs. into my shift. We talked for 9 hours, 37 min. I took one bathroom break about two hours in. Kara Levy [another team member] took care of me by bringing me food and drinks. We talked about life, movies, and favorite foods."[9] Labus explained, "Sometimes people just need to call and talk. We don't judge, we just want to help." The previous record had been eight hours and forty-seven minutes, set in 2011. There is no record that either customer bought anything on those calls.

At even the finest call center operations around the world, the person helping you on the phone needs to be mindful of his or her productivity, of the need to move on to the next call as soon as your needs are satisfied. Nowhere is the expression "time is money" more true than in the call center business. But not at Zappos. When you call Zappos, perhaps with questions about a pair of shoes or gloves, you are guaranteed to speak with someone who has only worthy intentions. You have the full attention of that Zappos employee, who has only your interests in mind, even if might take you nine hours to discuss it. Quite possibly no other company on earth shows as well that their pure expression of worthy intentions is so clearly a matter of corporate policy.

Members of Zappos' customer loyalty team sometimes send out personalized, handwritten notes to customers after sharing particularly meaningful conversations. If in the course of a discussion there is a mention of a birthday or anniversary coming up, the call reps are authorized to send flowers or Mrs. Fields cookies to customers. And if any Zappos-sold products break or tear, loyalty team members have the power to order a free replacement within a year of the sale.

In our retailer study, customers rated Zappos highly for its warmth-related dimension, such as its ability to resolve problems fairly and honestly. "Value" and "lowest prices" were rated only eighth and fourteenth in importance, respectively, by these customers. Zappos prices tend to be the same suggested retail prices as department stores. Customers come to Zappos for the experience, not to hunt for bargains. All told, 95 percent of Zappos sales are transacted online, without making a phone call. But when customers call, they get lots of opportunities to interact directly with Zappos employees, who are able to express worthy intentions and allow us as customers to experience their warmth and competence. As a result, Zappos generates 75 percent of its sales every day from repeat customers—with no need for discounts, mass advertising, or rewards-based "loyalty" programs. We know when we are really appreciated.

The Amazon Challenge

Zappos and Amazon are both big online retail brands that are achieving tremendous growth and customer loyalty in distinctly different ways. The most obvious difference between the two is their size. Amazon, like its namesake river, is a vast and sprawling force of nature, with $61 billion in annual sales. Zappos, on the other hand, is a wholly owned subsidiary of Amazon which operates independently and contributes about $1 billion to Amazon's annual revenues.

In Chris's retailer study, just 33 percent of adults reported shopping with Zappos, while 98 percent had bought something from Amazon. Unlike Zappos, Amazon was rated significantly higher on competence than on warmth, even though its warmth ratings were still surprisingly good. Nonetheless, the dimensions that customers rated most important when buying from Amazon were website reliability, wide selection, value, and lowest prices available.

That is the chief distinction between the Zappos approach and the Amazon approach to online commerce. Zappos charges higher prices but offers exceptional hands-on customer service. Amazon relies heavily on low prices to generate our purchases and loyalty, while minimizing direct contact with employees. Amazon often sells products below cost to generate traffic and revenue, which helps explain why, with $61 billion in revenue in 2012, Amazon recorded a loss for the year of $39 million.

Amazon's most amazing feat, perhaps, is that it has managed to earn such high ratings for warmth without offering customers any direct human contact. Amazon provides one of the best examples of how expert web design and high functionality can give us that sense of a website as a "social actor," as referenced earlier. In essence, Amazon expresses worthy intentions toward its customers by offering low prices and a highly responsive online shopping portal. Amazon helps us buy things cheaply and effortlessly. Interacting with the product selection and prices on the Amazon site is so gratifying that users infer the warmth of Amazon, its culture, and its employees. It is a striking example of how high competence can be used to express worthy intentions, which in turn generates our perceptions of Amazon's warmth, which in turn engenders loyalty.

The challenge Amazon faces, however, is as enormous as Amazon itself. Eventually, Amazon's double-digit rate of growth will slow and the company will have to raise prices to generate a reasonable and sustained profit. Because loyalty to Amazon is based substantially on its low prices, how long would that loyalty last if their pricing advantage disappeared?

Clues to the answer lie in Amazon's history of competition with Zappos. In 2006, Amazon launched Endless.com as a separate branded subsidiary to go head-to-head with Zappos and other sites selling shoes and handbags. Despite all the advantages of scale, low prices, and marketing power that parent Amazon offered, Endless.com failed to compete with Zappos. In 2009, Amazon announced it was buying Zappos for $1.2 billion.[10] Endless.com met its end in 2012 when Amazon shut it down and folded its operations under the Amazon brand.[11] Having failed to compete with Zappos, Amazon bought the company and, by all accounts, has allowed it to function as a separate unit with a customer-obsessed model for e-commerce distinctly different from its parent company's.

The Zappos model of e-commerce engenders customer loyalty that is impervious to pricing. That is the competitive advantage that Zappos will enjoy in the years to come. Zappos' leaders don't have to worry about being undercut on price because they don't rely much on pricing as their way of expressing worthy intentions to customers. Zappos customers would enjoy paying less, no doubt, but they're not about to abandon their relationships with the company over a few dollars.

Amazon's leadership, on the other hand, has plenty to worry about. Although Amazon remains a uniquely successful case of using high competence to develop a perception of warmth, the company ultimately exemplifies the fragility of competence as a positive attribute in the Relationship Renaissance. The customer who enjoys a pleasant chat with a Zappos rep or receives a card from her in the mail is not likely to retreat from that relationship and that highly satisfying experience, just to save some money. But Amazon's relationships are built upon the expectation that shopping with Amazon is faster, easier, *and* cheaper. If Amazon loses that last distinction in its attempt to earn some profits for its shareholders, it's likely to find that many of its customers had offered Amazon their loyalty solely because of Amazon's rock-bottom prices.

The Relational Upside

A 2011 study of global consumer behavior by Accenture points to some of the challenges that e-commerce must confront in the Relationship Renaissance.[12] The power of the customer is growing. "The satisfaction bar keeps rising," the Accenture report observed. Forty-four percent of respondents said that their expectations for customer satisfaction were higher than in the previous year. Only 8 percent had lower expectations.

Because of these rising expectations, the Accenture report revealed two seemingly conflicting developments. On one hand, customer satisfaction is climbing right along with customer expectations. On the other hand, customer loyalty is declining. The growth in customer power is driving both trends.

As measured by Accenture, customer satisfaction was up all across the board in 2011. Customers reported being much more satisfied, in particular, with employees who were polite, friendly, knowledgeable, and well-informed. Customers were also more satisfied with wait times than they were in 2010. And yet, Accenture reported that only one in four customers feel "very loyal" to their providers of goods and services, and many profess no feelings of loyalty at all. Two-thirds said they had abandoned a regular provider in the past year over the issue of poor customer service. It's as though the harder companies and brands work to make us happy, the more demanding we become.

The Digital Response

At the outset of the dot-com boom in the late 1990s, some argued that consumers would never buy certain products or services online because they could never be certain of who they were dealing with or whether they would get what they paid for. Now, ironically, the tables seem to have turned. Some of the same digital technologies regarded with such suspicion not that long ago are now leading the way when it comes to sustaining relational customer loyalty.

Most of us have learned through trial and error how to judge the warmth and competence of online sellers. We routinely transact business with people and things we cannot see or touch in person. In early 2013, the CEO of eBay claimed that the company was selling eight thousand cars per week through eBay's mobile app alone.[13] Who would have guessed a decade earlier that we would be using our phones to buy used cars from total strangers?

For all the distance and dehumanization that scalable technologies have contributed to commerce over the past 150 years, the silver lining may be this: some of those mass marketing innovations and technological advances can also help meet the rising expectations of the newly empowered customer. When companies and brands manage to balance the convenience and efficiency of e-commerce with personalized relationships buoyed by warmth and competence, we as customers can enjoy the benefits of low prices, wide selection, *and* personal service. It's a best-of-both worlds result that was impossible during the Middle Ages of Marketing.

Social networks—such as Facebook, Twitter, and Pinterest, along with all the mobile applications that are proliferating around them—make it possible for us to establish and maintain one-to-one interactions more efficiently and conveniently than ever before. Although short posts or Tweets have certain limits to what they can express, they allow us as customers to again interact directly with employees with real names and faces. The significance of this development cannot be overstated, particularly for companies and brands that have become highly digitized, automated, and outsourced. The significance for us as customers has become obvious, thanks to our warmth-and-competence-detecting brains.

A 2012 study by the Simply Measured consulting group showed that while nearly all of the companies represented by

the Interbrand 100 use Twitter accounts to broadcast marketing messages, twenty-three of the brands also maintain Twitter
accounts dedicated to handling customer service questions and
complaints.[14] These provide some of the best examples of the
relationship-building capabilities of social networks.

Meeting customer expectations for these accounts can
be a challenge, though, since 42 percent of customers expect
responses to their tweets within an hour, whereas 9 percent of
the brands say that their average response time meets those
expectations. Twitter accounts @NikeSupport and @AskAmex
are among those that attract the highest Twitter demand—more
than two hundred messages per day. They also manage average
response times of three hours or less.

These personalized interactions allow companies and brands
to express their worthy intentions (and allow us to detect their
warmth and competence) in ways that are easier for us to process and recall. What's more, when these interactions take place
within a social network, they are just a click away from being
shared by customers with all of their friends and followers.

The potential for that "viral" network effect also shows why
a Twitter account of this kind needs to be handled with care.
"Twitter provides instant gratification for the info-junkie," Simply
Measured's report points out, "so it's only natural that users would
expect the same from their customer service experience . . . A late
reply can mean the difference between a happy return customer
and a bitter consumer rapid-firing complaints about your brand."[15]

There is enormous potential for Facebook and Twitter to
help companies and brands establish and maintain these kinds
of direct relationships with us as their customers. Even as companies and brands begin to realize the vast relationship management capabilities of these networks, they commonly refer to
both as "social *media*," as though they are just another place
to post advertising banners and promotional offers. As customers,
we know better.

Missed Opportunities

During the heyday of the Industrial Revolution, producers understandably lost direct contact with our grandparents as end customers. It was physically and technologically impossible for them to have direct contact with one another. Mass market advertising was created as the only practical and available way for producers to communicate with large numbers of current or potential customers.

Today, given the digital revolution, it's just foolish and lazy for them to keep us at arm's length. Mass market advertising, for that reason, has continued far beyond its point of diminishing returns. It represents the old, lazy, and wasteful way to communicate indiscriminately with everyone.

Advertisers, however, are loath to send mass media gently into its good night. Chris once sat in on a work session with members of a national association of major advertisers on a mission to co-opt the Internet and social networks. The association had retained a large consulting firm to help establish an online equivalent to the Nielsen TV ratings system. The idea was to create a stable and universally accepted means for pricing and monitoring the delivery of banner and video advertising, so that a "television-like" order could be established in the chaotic online advertising world.

It would have been comical if there hadn't been so much at stake. Technologies like the Internet and social networks have finally made it possible to escape the mass advertising ways of the Middle Ages of Marketing in favor of one-to-one interactions, but all those who are vested in and comfortable with those old advertising ways are trying desperately to hold on to the past. They want to turn the Internet and social networks into an online version of television.

Rather than trying to minimize interactions between humans through automation, companies and brands should be seeking to maximize those interactions using technology, so that their warmth and competence can be displayed and customer relationships established with us. The Internet and social networks have made it possible once again for the employees of companies and brands to have direct, interactive conversations with customers in a way that is efficient, scalable, and trackable.

If companies and brands were to fully recognize and embrace how we purchase and become loyal to them, they would use social networks more effectively as the relationship management systems they are ideally suited to be. They can and should present themselves as human brands that treat us as human beings.

The social networks themselves are partly responsible for the confusion that reigns today. Most of them make it too difficult for companies and brands to use them for maintaining dialogues with their customers. For example, it would be great if we customers could ask a question or register a complaint with an employee who is known to us by name and face, directly from the company Facebook page. But Facebook permits only one voice—the administrator's voice—for each page representing a company or brand. So we are left to talk to a faceless monolith—which often isn't the company or brand anyway, but rather a digital marketing agency hired to keep us away from their client.

Any number of loyalty insights and metrics would be available to allow companies to communicate with us, if only these social networks were configured and leveraged to enable them. What better way is there to get to know us as people and what we care about than our social network profiles? What better and more convenient place is there to ask us for feedback on problem resolution and how much warmth and competence we see in them and how much loyalty we feel toward them?

Doing these things would give companies not only the means to conduct a trackable dialogue with us but also a great opportunity to measure, manage, and strengthen their relational loyalty with us. Given everything customers say in the research, these direct human interactions would surely convey more warmth and competence than faceless automated messages carried over from the Middle Ages of Marketing.

Chapter Five

Take Us to Your Leader

What we learn from the people behind the things we buy

Back in 2009, Domino's Pizza was in the final stages of a chain-wide makeover with an entirely new set of recipes for its hand-tossed pizza. When it came time to shoot commercials in support of the new "Pizza Turnaround" campaign, Domino's ad agency didn't prepare a script or audition any actors. Instead, a documentary film crew was hired to interview Domino CEO Patrick Doyle, the company's head chef Brandon Solano, and a handful of other company employees. In their own words, each of them expressed to the camera the same direct, disarming sentiment: "We're sorry our old pizza wasn't very good."[1]

Long before the ad campaign had been conceived, Domino's chief marketing officer, Russell Weiner, recognized that despite some improvements over the years, the quality of their pizza had not kept pace with customers' growing expectations. The Domino's team invested in two years of testing with countless combinations of ingredients to completely reinvent its pizza from scratch. In the end, they were able to create a pizza that testing showed was preferred over all competitors' offerings by a wide margin.

As Weiner contemplated how to introduce Domino's new pizza recipe, he understood he faced a challenge in breaking through to customers who had grown accustomed to Domino's mediocre fare. Weiner had even googled the phrase "new and improved," turning up millions of hits. "It made me realize," he told Chris in an interview, "we can't just come out and say, 'Hey, we have a new and improved pizza!' It would be such a wasted opportunity."[2]

Instead, Domino's executives decided that they would introduce their new pizza by first apologizing sincerely for their old pizza. And that apology would come from the top. According to the Domino's ad agency, "[W]e had Domino's CEO and other executives tell their own story of how they changed the pizza. This contributed to the honesty and the transparency that made the campaign so powerful."[3]

After the documentary crew was finished, Weiner had the new commercials tested in advance of their debut during the December 2009 NFL playoffs. That's when he knew that Domino's message would strike a nerve with viewers. Test viewers gave the ads some of the highest marks ever garnered by a fast-food commercial. "It was by far, *by far*, off the charts," Weiner said.[4]

Almost immediately after its launch, "Domino's Pizza Turnaround" proved to be one of the most successful restaurant ad campaigns of all time. Same-store sales at Domino's increased 14.3 percent during the first quarter of 2010, the largest single-quarter gain in the entire history of fast food.[5] In 2009, Domino's had lagged in growth behind almost all its competitors, but Domino's revenues in 2010 climbed faster than those of any other U.S. quick-serve restaurant chain, including McDonald's and Starbucks.[6] "People said to us, 'Oh, did you spend more money?'" Weiner recalls. "Believe it or not, the year we launched the new pizza, we spent *less* money than the prior year. It's just that the work was so powerful, it seemed like we were hitting [the airwaves] more."[7]

Doyle, for his part, told *QSR* magazine in 2012 that he decided to appear in the Domino's ads because he knew that his presence would help the message break through. "When the CEO of a company goes out and says our old pizza wasn't very good, you're going to get breakthrough," he said.[8] In 2011, a survey by Zeta Interactive named Doyle one of its "Top Ten Most Buzzed-About CEOs" for the year.[9]

Doyle and Domino's are unusual in that most companies would rather that we *never* buzz about their CEOs. The main reason is that whenever there's CEO buzz, there's a good chance the buzz is bad. CEOs often make the biggest headlines of their careers by saying things they wish they hadn't. Consider the controversial comments of Chick-fil-A COO Dan Cathy about gay marriage[10] and Whole Foods CEO John Mackey's remarks equating Obamacare with fascism.[11] The CEO in each of these cases managed to alienate many people who might otherwise have become or remained satisfied customers, while distracting his management team and employees from more important concerns.

Normally, most CEOs enter the limelight only when forced by disaster or threat of disaster. That's when, under the stress of fluid circumstances, poor phrasing can become almost as big a problem as the problem itself. Whether it's BP's Tony Hayward whining about wanting his life back or Bank of America's Brian Moynihan feebly claiming his bank's "right to make a profit," such gaffes are commonly held out as reasons why senior executives should stay away from the public and the media. Conventional wisdom in corporate communications says that top leaders should be kept away from public view because the risk is too great that they will embarrass themselves and the company.

Social media in particular is seen as a growing threat in this respect. "Advertising in the YouTube age can be a dangerous forum for the boss to personally deliver the brand's message," one veteran ad exec told *Advertising Age* in 2009. "You'd better be sure your CEO is capable and believable, and that his or her message is likable and worth watching before you put him or her in front of the camera and in the line of fire from digital tomato throwers."[12] That might have been wise advice during the Middle Ages of Marketing, but the mobile, social, and digital age leaves no place for CEOs to hide. They might as well get used to public exposure, even if, on occasion, they're required to duck some "digital tomatoes."

It is in our human nature to seize on gaffes and misstatements from powerful business leaders. They burn in our memories because such offhand remarks by CEOs in particular offer a rare glimpse into the true intentions of the powerful companies and brands they lead. Just as we are compelled to judge companies and brands as though they were actually people, we base those judgments on what we know or can infer about the real people behind each company—their warmth and competence and hence the warmth and competence of that company.

So when we hear Dan Cathy's religious objections to gay marriage, some of us wonder if it is evidence that Chick-fil-A's management culture might be similarly intolerant of other social groups. For others, though, the comment might reflect evidence of a company devoted to "traditional values." John Mackey's principled distaste for federal regulation of health care might make some of us wonder whether he is also dismissive of other federal regulations—wage regulations, food regulations—that might cast doubt on the soundness of Whole Foods' operations. We consider such questions because it's in our nature to wonder how the words of anyone with power will affect us.[13] We try to infer from their comments how their warmth and competence, and their true intentions, might have consequences for our own lives.

The Pizza Turnaround

By admitting on national television that they all need to improve at serving and satisfying customers, Patrick Doyle and his team provided Domino's customers with a surprisingly candid show of emotion. That such a distinctively open and honest approach resulted in the greatest single-quarter revenue gain in fast-food history is an impressive testament to the power of expressing one's worthy intentions. Pizza Turnaround did much more than arouse customer interest in a new pizza recipe. The ad acknowledged poor past performance and requested forgiveness. Customers could accept the apology by picking up their phones and trying the new recipe. Millions of them did.

The quality we find so appealing when we encounter authentic emotions on the faces of people behind otherwise faceless corporations is what social psychologists call "concreteness."[14] In most of our interactions with companies and brands, concreteness is absent. Instead, we engage in an exchange based on abstractions, which direct our general behavior (making purchases) but tend not to engender true loyalty. For instance, prior to Pizza Turnaround, nearly everyone experienced the Domino's brand as a set of abstract symbols and metaphors—televised ad images of steaming pizzas, the distinctive red-white-and-blue box, the domino logo, and the famed reputation for speedy delivery.

Once Domino's ads involved candid, unscripted footage of some the company's top people (as opposed to logos and images of pizza), customers could enjoy the concrete experience of their personal warmth and competence: their worthy intentions. That, in turn, gave customers access to more *specific* feelings toward the company, increasing the odds they would take more specific actions to support the brand, such as endorsing the new pizza to friends or discussing the commercials with workmates.

This is why loyalty to people, even as televised images, is more concrete and authentic than loyalty to a company or brand. When we watch head chef Brandon Solano introduce a new product in a Domino's commercial, we're watching him ask us to give his latest creation a chance, and to give *him* another chance, too. Thanks to his televised *mea culpa*, we want to give him that chance, because we know him as someone who deserves it. With this concrete experience, the mere act of ordering a pizza can become a way to support a good person who has demonstrated worthy intentions in the form of both warmth and competence toward us.

Not much in this dynamic seems very rational. Domino's millions of customers don't actually know Patrick Doyle and Brandon Solano at all. But by speaking the truth in their own words on the air, by expressing their desire to please and showing us their chagrined faces, Doyle and his team stir something primal inside us. We want to trust the words and faces of such people. We have a human need to do so, and we feel good about ourselves when we offer them our support. Any group, any "tribe," that demonstrates their worthy intentions in such a remarkable way appeals to us as deserving of our respect. Of course, their well-intentioned words must be backed up with competent follow-through. The new pizza had better taste good. But if they deliver on their apologetic promises, our trust in them feels validated, and our loyalty grows and deepens as a result.

For decades, the business establishment has doubted the wisdom of using CEOs in advertising, although that skepticism just may be lifting. Studies by AceMetrix show that generally CEO ads rank above average in their effectiveness when compared with other advertising.[15] Although not all CEO ads are successful, AceMetrix found that the most effective CEO ads deliver messages that are "direct, trust-inspiring," "communicate a no-nonsense style," and show the CEO to be "genuine and authentic." (All of these adjectives, by the way, connote either warmth or competence.) The report stated that the most effective current CEO spokespeople are John Schnatter of Papa John's Pizza and Jim Koch of Sam Adams Beer. Each company is notable for fully embracing what the report called a long-term "CEO-as-pitchman" advertising strategy.

These results are very different from what AceMetrix discovered about a far more popular advertising tactic: the celebrity endorsement. In a 2011 report, AceMetrix revealed testing results showing that celebrity ads were outperformed by *non*-celebrity ads in all demographics, regardless of age or gender.[16] Billions are spent each year on celebrity endorsements and sponsorships, even though they produce poor results virtually across the board.

AceMetrix found that sole exception to this rule was Oprah Winfrey. Ads for a car insurance company featuring Winfrey tested "spectacularly," AceMetrix found, when compared with other insurance industry spots. The report notes, however, that none of Winfrey's ads portrayed her as actually endorsing an insurance product. Instead, the ads were cause-themed. They addressed public safety issues such as the dangers of texting while driving. So although Winfrey was unique among celebrities for her high-scoring ads, it seems likely they scored high because she didn't try to sell anything to her millions of fans. The ads were merely vehicles for her to express her worthy intentions about her fans' physical safety.[17]

It's hard to see a role for celebrity endorsements in the ongoing Relationship Renaissance. Because celebrities rarely have much to do with the warmth and competence of the brands they represent, by definition they lack the authenticity that we demand in commercial messaging. On the other hand, it is highly likely that we will see more companies "Doing a Domino's" (as acts of public apology were sometimes called when Patrick Doyle's ads first hit the air). That's because our expectations for getting to know the people behind companies and brands are rising like never before. Research by Euro RSCG shows that most Americans now say they want companies "to be open to dialogue with them and to be totally transparent." But the public also believes that most leaders lack the capacity to deliver on such goals. Less than 20 percent of survey respondents say that they admire business leaders more today than they used to—admiration being the prized emotion that is evoked by combined warmth and competence.[18]

So the need is growing for more leaders who can be genuine, transparent, and accessible to us. Notice that neither John

Schnatter nor Jim Koch possesses a particularly riveting or dynamic television persona. They are credible and inspiring CEO-spokesmen only because they capably express their sincere and passionate desire to serve their customers' best interests and to lead others to deliver consistently on that promise. In fact, if either of them were more glib and polished, we might regard them as less than genuine and not so trustworthy. The depth of their commitment to the everyday reality of serving us is far more important than any excitement they might project on-screen. By acting as the "face" of their respective companies and brands, they offer us a sense of emotional reassurance as living embodiments of the company's trustworthiness, warmth, and competence.

The increasingly impersonal nature of commerce is starving us of this sense of reassurance. Technology keeps making it easier for us to transact business without human interaction. E-commerce is displacing retail stores at a growing clip, and one of the largest trends among traditional retailers is the self-service checkout counter. In such an environment, we are bound to grow more cautious and less loyal toward companies and brands whose leaders remain hidden behind logos, advertising, and automation. The need has never been greater for corporate leaders such as Doyle, Schnatter, and Koch—CEOs who want our loyalty and offer us concrete demonstrations of their warmth and competence in order to get it.

Transformational Leadership

It may seem neither reasonable nor logical to judge a company or brand by whether you like its CEO as a spokesperson. But just as we have a primal desire to judge brands by the people behind them, no single individual represents those people more prominently than the CEO. There is no avoiding how deeply we take such leadership cues to our hearts. We want to believe that what is true about any leader is likely also true about his or her followers. So if leadership is to gain the spotlight more often in the Relationship Renaissance, then our concept of leadership itself needs to shift accordingly.

Bernard M. Bass's famous 1990 leadership study looked at this subject from the standpoint of "heroes, leadership prototypes, and charisma."[19] In Bass's estimation, there are two kinds of corporate leadership. The first, *transactional* leadership, is based on rational, economic-choice types of exchanges between leaders and employees. It is an "if-it-ain't-broke-don't-fix-it" approach found most often among the big bureaucratic corporations that Tom Peters famously regarded as "dinosaurs."

The second kind, *transformational* leadership, occurs when leaders stir their employees to look beyond their own self-interest for the good of the group. Bass concluded that transformational leaders are much more productive because their inspiring leadership prompts employees to exert extra effort on their behalf. Companies led by transformational leaders tend to outperform others due to the tendency of lower-level employees to imitate the characteristics of the leader above them. Psychologically, we are all prone to playing follow-the-leader. That is why Bass invoked Napoleon's observation that an army of rabbits led by a lion would defeat an army of lions led by a rabbit.[20] Bass also wrote that transformational leadership is particularly important whenever a firm faces a turbulent marketplace. On the other hand, although he regarded transactional leadership as a recipe for mediocrity, Bass found that it still had a place in what he called "stable organizations" that are unaffected by marketplace disruptions. Decades later, though, it's hard to find an industry that is *not* facing a turbulent marketplace. Transactional leadership, most highly developed among Tom Peters's "dinosaurs," seems destined to go the way of all dinosaurs.

We all need to be inspired by transformational leadership. This is the lesson that corporate governing boards must take to heart immediately, after years of trying to hide their leaders from public

view. Many business executives today lack this capacity for transformation because they were hired to make money, not to build
loyal long-term relationships with their customers. Such leaders,
lacking in warmth and worthy intentions toward their customers,
will inevitably demonstrate that their transactional style makes
them incompetent to lead in a new, transparent, transformational
century. The speed of change is so great that companies and brands
should take care now to make sure that the people who get their
top job in the first place are capable of expressing their worthy
intentions, and in full view of all their customers.

Come Out from Behind the Curtain

If there were ever a company that needed transformation, it was
Domino's in 2009. The longtime leader in delivery pizza found
itself in the embarrassing and unusual position of being rated
above all its competitors for service and speed of delivery, but at
the very bottom for taste and quality.[21]

By pulling off the Pizza Turnaround in 2010, however,
Domino's demonstrated just how quickly a direct display of
warmth and competence can change public perception of a
mature multi-billion-dollar company. Having won the distinction
as the nation's fastest-growing quick-serve restaurant chain that
year, the inevitable question that arose was, how long before the
magic would wear off?

"Everyone thought we'd be down in 2011," Russell Weiner
recalls. "But we were up 3.5 percent."[22] This was because Domino's
extended its campaign for additional transparency. It brought out
more faces from behind the curtain. One documentary-style commercial featured the company's "chicken chef," Tate Dillow. When
Tate is presented with the new cardboard containers that his ten-
ders are to be delivered in, the cameras capture his shock at seeing
his own name printed on the sides. Also on the box was a simple
question for customers: "Did we get it right?" followed by three

check boxes: "Nope." "Almost." "Oh Yes We Did." CEO Doyle says to the camera, referring to Dillow's chicken recipe, "I think it's great, but it's not great until our customers tell us it's great."[23]

The success of the new pizza campaign persuaded Domino's executives that, in Weiner's words, "You don't need to do this only when you make a mistake." The company had resorted to warts-and-all transparency as a tactic to break through the noise of commercial clutter. But then transparency evolved into one of Domino's guiding corporate strategies. In everything Domino's does, the company looks for ways to involve its customers, deal openly with mistakes, and engender customer loyalty.

An online Domino's pizza tracker lets you watch online to see where your pizza order is at the moment: in the oven, in the box, or on its way. A feedback function on the tracker allows you to post what you think of your pizza, so everyone can see how Domino's is faring. For a time, Domino's arranged to have the tracker postings appear in a live crawl on an electronic billboard in Times Square.[24] (The comments, Weiner says, were about 85 percent positive.[25])

Domino's also did away with the most casually accepted form of consumer fraud in the restaurant advertising world: "food styling." That's the name for the photographic art of making fast food in advertising appear much more appealing than what's actually served.

"We've sworn off food styling," Weiner explains.[26] Now, whenever you see a picture of Domino's pizza, it was most likely taken by a fan with a cellphone camera. Domino's invites customers to upload shots of their food to be publicly posted on the company's Facebook site.[27] Most pictures are of happy little children posing with their pizza slices, but one customer posed while dangling off a cliff clad in full rappelling gear, an opened box of Domino's in one hand.[28] A Georgia woman photographed her pizza next to her enormously pregnant bare belly. Written in marker, with a comic-strip bubble pointing to her navel, was a message from the baby: "I want Domino's pizza!"[29]

Then one day, "one of the pictures that we got was a pretty bad picture of our pizza," Weiner says. "It wasn't delivered the right way, and rather than hiding it, we put it on national television." In that commercial, a pained-looking Patrick Doyle points to a photo of gooey cheese and toppings stuck to the inside top of a Domino's box and says, "This is not acceptable. Bryce, from Minnesota, you shouldn't have to get this from Domino's. We're better than this." He admits that seeing the picture "really gets me upset," and promises, "We're not going to deliver pizzas like this. I guarantee it . . . We're going to learn. We're going to get better."[30]

The Minnesota franchisee who served up the infamous bad pizza is now aware that the company CEO is personally monitoring the store's performance. "What it does, it makes you a better company," Weiner says of Domino's commitment to transparency. "Not only because our customers feel like we're doing stuff for them, but when we showed the picture of the bad pizza on the air, guess what? Our people were that much more careful when they made and delivered pizzas . . . I basically have three hundred million people mystery-shopping for me."[31]

Remember the warning about "digital tomato-throwers" mentioned earlier in the chapter? Leave it to a delivery pizza company to take those tossed tomatoes and make tomato sauce.

At the Heart of Loyalty

A consistent approach to communicating worthy intentions of this kind ultimately transforms a company's ability to influence its customers. Researchers describe three types of influence we experience that constitute three processes of attitude change.[32] The most fundamental force of influence is compliance. We comply with a requirement in order to achieve a desired result (we pay taxes to avoid punishment). Then there are two higher forms of influence, the ones through which we form emotional bonds and loyalty attachments: *identification* (we pay taxes because that's what we all do as Americans), and *internalization* (we pay taxes because it's the right thing to do).

Prior to 2010, customers were influenced to buy Domino's pizza almost entirely on the basis of compliance. For a competitive price, customers enjoyed hot food, delivered to their doors. Domino's had little to work with as far as inspiring true loyalty from its customers through the influence of identification or internalization.

But once the Domino's team apologized and promised to do better, which demonstrated their loyalty to the customer first, it was as though Patrick Doyle had invited us to be inspired by his brave example (identification) and to share his personal values of respect, honesty, and integrity (internalization). The connection with customers that Domino's achieved through its ads and online activities created a whole new value proposition for customers. Instead of merely getting cheap, filling pizza delivered at a good price, we may actually feel like we want to support and reward the CEO and his company—assuming, of course, that the food really does taste better.

The magic of such a turnaround, and other success stories like it, is how we can form deeper bonds with a company along all three lines of compliance in a single transaction. You may order Domino's though compliance because you're hungry and it's a good price for good pizza. At that same time, you can enjoy certain feelings of identification, because you see something of yourself in the CEO's down-to-earth worthy intentions, and still other feelings of internalization, because you take some pleasure in supporting companies you admire. That kind of loyalty attachment can never be formed through clever advertising with celebrity spokespersons.

Leading by Example

Earlier chapters discussed how the human face was the first "brand logo"; how the face is a powerful medium, capable of conveying identity, personality, intentions, and ability all at once, in an instant. We are drawn to companies and brands that provide us with a visible leader, someone whose face we can relate to, onto whom we can project all our assumptions about the organizations they lead. Our minds crave making this connection.

Oprah Winfrey, Steve Jobs, Sam Walton, and Richard Branson are just a few of the most obvious and compelling examples of celebrity CEOs who have invited us to identify with them and internalize their values, so that buying their products is something more than a simple economic exchange. When we consider the most fanatically loyal customers of the Oprah Winfrey Network, of Apple, of Wal-Mart, or of Virgin, these leaders' images, expressed by their faces, can become a stand-in for what is known as the company's "prototype" ideal.[33]

When PepsiCo CEO Indra Nooyi sat for interviews in 2011 to support the company's worldwide Pepsi Refresh Project to give away $20 million in grants to improve communities, she appeared on media outlets such as CNN and CNBC with the intention of representing that elevated role, giving her thoughts on job creation, healthier snacks, and her personal work-life balance. "She wasn't talking about earnings-per-share, she wasn't talking about growth rates" recalls Tim Cost, the current president of Jacksonville University who was then Nooyi's executive vice-president of Global Corporate Affairs. "She was delivering warmer messages."[34]

Nooyi has also spoken at the South by Southwest conference and is one of the few CEOs to give a TED talk. "The TED talk had nothing to do with PepsiCo," Cost explains. "It had to do with how to take the Pepsi Refresh concept and extend it into the education space. How do we use the best and brightest people we know to help education? To me, she is the most extraordinary warmth generator for consumers, because when you let people watch her, people like her, believe her, and trust her."[35]

Research on group dynamics shows that when we all share the same in-group values—by believing that we all, in our in-group, are warm and competent—then the person who leads us represents the most extreme ideal of that commonly held concept of warmth and competence.[36, 37] We don't want to be led by the person who possesses only the group's average values; that person seems uninspiring; better than some, worse than others. Instead, we expect leaders be at the extreme high end of commitment to the group's collective ideal of itself. That's why we use physical terms when speaking of such a person: someone who *embodies* the group's values, who is the public *face* of the company. The person we follow as a leader must represent its ideals in their highest expression, its very heart and soul.

Such highly visible and outspoken business leaders make it easy and enjoyable to grow loyal attachments to their companies and brands. They provide us with a reassuring human face that represents the company's intentions toward us. Intentions, however, are only that. For us to gain a concrete sense of leaders' true abilities to act on their intentions, they must translate those intentions into actions and demonstrate them for all to see. And then they must be about to tell us all about it, in ways we can understand and appreciate.

Tell Us Your Story

Hershey's Chocolate, as described in Chapter One, is arguably one of America's most admired and beloved brands. In the research we conducted on Hershey's, we found, nonetheless, that most Americans don't know much at all about Hershey's considerable philanthropic activities. Susan and Chris conducted a survey to discover what effect such information might have on Hershey's brand loyalty.[38]

We told the survey respondents stories about Hershey's founding and its long heritage of philanthropy. The survey respondents already showed a strong brand preference for Hershey's prior to hearing these stories, but measures of brand purchase intent and brand loyalty went up significantly once they understood the worthy intentions behind the Hershey's brand, told in story form.

Stories organize our perceptions of the people, places, and events around us. Stories inform us emotionally, which is why we remember them better than mere information. They are among most powerful means of human communication, education, and inspiration, precisely because they overlap in our minds with our ways of making sense of other people.[39] Most of the brands that are greatly admired in warmth and competence terms have stories that express that warmth and competence in memorable ways.

Characters in every company's story—such as the Panera Bread manager, Honest Tea's founders, and Domino's CEO—define themselves by the actions they choose to take. They assert what is most important to them by making difficult choices in the face of considerable pressure to take the easier way out. It's that single quality—of a risky, character-defining choice made under pressure—that makes any good story register with us as concrete, emotional, meaningful, and memorable.

Nothing better conveys the identity and character of a leader and the warmth and competence of the company or brand he or she leads than the genuine story of their journey together serving customers. Learning about the background of the leaders of companies and brands conveys tremendous insight into where they are coming from, where they are headed, and how their choices and decisions will affect us.

We like underdog stories best of all, which is why so many upstart brands promote the charming stories of their humble beginnings. Some companies, eBay most prominent among them, go so far as to generate "creation myths" about their origins in hope of inspiring customers and earning media attention. From a credibility and transparency standpoint, this is a terrible practice that can backfire easily. EBay had to endure a round of negative publicity when the myth it had been promoting—that its founder invented the online auction site to help his girlfriend sell off her

Pez dispenser collection—turned out to have been invented by a junior public relations writer.[40] But deceptions of this kind are worth mentioning because they testify to the lengths to which some will go just to be identified as underdogs.

The appeal of the underdog story has deep psychological roots. Underdogs are attractive to us because we believe they need us. We feel we can count on them to do the right thing because they are a little desperate for our support and loyalty. How many times have we seen leaders choose the path of warmth and competence only when they were staring failure in the face, because nothing else had worked? Dan Hesse at Sprint discovered the enormous savings earned from good customer service only after Sprint had burned away billions of dollars with bad customer service. Zappos was rapidly running out of cash when Tony Hsieh resorted to a customer service–centered strategy. Domino's endured several years of flat growth and low customer satisfaction before it completely reinvented its recipes from scratch and conceived an ad campaign that began with humble apologies. Patrick Doyle told an interviewer that when one of Domino's top franchisees asked him what would happen if Pizza Turnaround failed, "All I could do was laugh and say, 'My successor will have a really hard time dealing with that.' There was no Plan B. There couldn't be. On the plus side, when you're facing something like that, it does tend to help you focus more."[41]

The old Avis slogan, "We're number two, so we try harder" makes a lot of sense to us, at least if we can safely assume that number two is just as competent as number one. The underdog always has something to prove, so we can count on the underdog's loyalty. Underdogs, we feel, will not abandon us in times of trouble. The only cautionary note is that not all underdogs are the same. Researchers studying sports fans have discovered, for instance, that in a contest involving two teams toward whom we feel no particular loyalty, we most likely choose to root for the team that oddsmakers predict will lose—technically, the underdog.[42]

However, not all predicted losers are underdogs. Research tells us that we have affection for a disfavored team only if that team is also the team with fewer resources, or one from a smaller-market city. If the team expected to lose happens to have a higher payroll, we don't perceive it as being an underdog. After all, where's the fun in rooting for a team of overpaid and underperforming athletes? A team that has the resources to win, but hasn't managed them well enough to win, is more likely to become an object of our contempt, for being both incompetent and unlovable.

What is the relevance of this research to companies and brands? Just that many brands need to be wary of being seen as being too big and too rich to be admired. A lot of so-called underdog brands are not really underdogs at all. Zappos and Honest Tea are just two upstart companies that have maintained their scrappy, underdog edge even though they are well-financed by wealthy parent companies.

Some of these companies go to greater lengths than most to conceal their corporate parentage, while telling stories about themselves that continue to speak to the underdog ideal. Ben & Jerry's Ice Cream, for instance, has been owned by the giant Anglo-Dutch conglomerate Unilever since the year 2000.[43] However, on the homespun, cartoonish Ben & Jerry's "Timeline" web page, the only significant event listed for the company in 2000 was 380,000 scoops of free ice cream given out at "Charity Scooper Bowls."[44] The timeline begins, naturally, with a panel called "Humble Beginnings," describing how Ben & Jerry's was started in 1978 thanks to a $5 ice cream–making correspondence course from Penn State.[45] The story of how Ben and Jerry turned that $5 investment into a $326 million payday from Unilever[46] is an awe-inspiring tale, but if it appeared on their website, it would not help build loyalty to the company and its products. The fact of Ben & Jerry's tremendous wealth would more likely elicit empty feelings of envy from customers, rather than warmth, competence, and admiration.

David versus Goliath

Few celebrity CEOs have better underdog stories to tell than Sir Richard Branson, billionaire chairman of the Virgin Group and, in 2013, the fourth-wealthiest person in Great Britain. Born in 1950 to a middle-class family in Surrey, England, Branson struggled with dyslexia all through his early years. He was even physically beaten by his boarding school teachers for failing to complete his written assignments. Eventually he dropped out of school altogether at the age of sixteen.

Despite his struggles with reading and math (to this day he cannot read a spreadsheet), Branson was a tenacious salesman and managed to start a successful London youth-culture magazine in 1966 when he was still just sixteen. By 1972, he'd parlayed his holdings into a mail-order record company, a record store, and a recording label, all of which went by the name Virgin. Branson went on to sign such acts as the Sex Pistols and the Rolling Stones, leading Virgin Music to grow from nothing to one of the six largest record companies in the world. After leaving the recording industry, Branson went on to found dozens of other Virgin-branded companies, most notably Virgin Airlines.

The tale of Branson's first ad hoc foray into the airline business in 1978 is a scrappy underdog story, even though Branson was already wealthy at the time. Branson and his wife were vacationing on tiny Beef Island in the Caribbean when they discovered that their scheduled flight to Puerto Rico had been canceled. Standing amid dozens of other stranded travelers in the airport terminal, Branson called around to charter companies and agreed to charter a flight for $2,000. He wrote in big letters on a blackboard in the terminal, "Virgin Airways: $39 single flight to Puerto Rico," and then he circulated through the crowd, collecting fares until the flight was filled. Six years later, he and a partner started Virgin Atlantic service between London and New York.

Branson's Virgin Group is a unique entity, a branded venture capital investment firm. Its dozens of companies also include Virgin Mobile, Virgin Wines, Virgin Festivals, Virgin Vacations, and Virgin Trains. Each company is a separately organized partnership, but all are united by the distinctive logic with which they enter and disrupt industries under the Virgin flag. In Branson's words: "We look for the big bad wolves who are dramatically overcharging and under-delivering."[47] Branson, the childhood underdog, is a billionaire today who heads a vast portfolio of underdog upstarts. He relishes playing the role of warm and competent David to the cold, lumbering Goliaths of the world, perhaps because of his own difficult childhood, but also because he understands the natural love that people have for smaller, eager newcomers. "Obviously, the David image has done Virgin no harm," he once said. "And if we ever became a Goliath, I think another David would set up and take us on."[48]

One of Branson's favorite methods of promoting the Virgin brand is to tackle death-defying, world-record-breaking stunts, all of which help promote the Virgin underdog story. He set a world record for the fastest crossing of the Atlantic in a small powerboat. He and a friend were the first men to cross both the Atlantic and Pacific oceans by balloon while riding in a tiny pressurized capsule. He even set a speed record for crossing the English Channel in an undersized amphibious vehicle. All of his daredevil attempts bear the Virgin brand name and create a narrative that reflects the Virgin mission. In each case, he and his small crew are set against some much larger force of nature, casting Branson in the heroic role of conquering what most people would be afraid even to contemplate.

Branson has built the Virgin empire more or less on this principle. He creates drama with his highly publicized stunts, and when announcing his latest underdog foray into a new industry, he always tells a story that tracks with the story we love most, of a David setting out to win our loyalty by bringing low yet another faceless industry Goliath. And Branson tells these stories himself because he's long been one of the most media-friendly and media-accessible CEOs in the world. Once, when told by a BBC producer that ninety-nine out of one hundred British CEOs decline invitations to appear on television, Branson responded, "From a competitive point of view, the longer they continue to think that way, the better for us."

Humans crave the heroes, villains, and emotional catharses provided by storytellers like Branson. Stories provide a healthy workout for our warmth and competence muscles, offering adventures, experiences, and emotions that we don't usually have access to in our daily lives. They provide social currency, access to a shared sense of identity, and escape from the confines of our own daily concerns.

On a Saturday evening in February 2007, a high-speed Virgin Train carrying 120 passengers derailed in the remote Cumbria region of England, killing an eighty-year-old woman. Prior to that day, Virgin's planes and trains had carried a half-billion passengers without a fatality, and Branson looked shaken on SkyNews as he surveyed the wreckage of his first transportation disaster.[49] Having left a family vacation to show up on the scene, he pronounced it "a very sad day because of the loss of one life and the injuries caused to other people."[50]

Branson was generous in his praise of police, military, and emergency personnel who rushed to the scene. He lauded the train's engineer, who was badly injured, for his heroism in trying to slow the train and reduce the impact of the crash. He even praised the train car's design and expressed hope that its roll-cage construction had perhaps prevented greater loss of life. Then Branson visited hospitals to check up on the injured. Although investigations would later show that fault for the derailment lay with the company responsible for maintaining that stretch of track, there is no mention of the track maintenance company's CEO coming to the scene that day.[51]

Leaders like Richard Branson, who spend time in front of the curtain telling true stories about how they put their customers first, are able to draw on the years of credibility they have banked with the public when facing days like this one. Sooner or later, the leader of almost every organization will be thrust into the spotlight of public attention, because even well-managed companies and brands make mistakes and experience accidents. And when that happens, customers and the broader public will judge the intentions and abilities of that entire organization based on the warmth and competence that is conveyed by that leader's words and actions. If a CEO in such a situation has been hidden from public sight prior to that day, it is human nature for us to be suspicious of his or her intentions—as the next chapter will show.

Chapter Six

Show Your True Colors

*Why mistakes and crises are a golden
loyalty opportunity*

On August 28, 2009, a forty-five-year-old California Highway
Patrol officer named Mark Saylor brought his 2006 Lexus to
a San Diego-area Toyota dealership for repairs to the CD player,
parking brake, and console lighting. The dealership loaned Saylor
a 2009 Lexus ES 350 for the day, and he drove off, along with his
wife, brother-in-law, and teenage daughter.[1]

As Saylor drove the loaner Lexus down Route 125 in sub-
urban San Diego, the car's accelerator suddenly jammed. The
vehicle kept going faster, no matter how hard Saylor pumped the
brakes, until it reached speeds later calculated between 112 and
150 miles per hour.[2] Saylor's panicked brother-in-law called 911
to report that the Lexus had lost its brakes and was out of control. On the audiotape later released to the public, Saylor can be
heard in the background, telling his passengers to "hold on" and
"pray."[3] At Mission Gorge Road, where the Route 125 freeway

abruptly ends, the Lexus struck an SUV, rolled over at least twice and landed upside down in a dry riverbed, where it burst into flames. Everyone in the car was killed.

The crash investigation showed evidence that with the throttle fully opened on the 272-horsepower Lexus engine, the car's brake surfaces had been melted by Saylor's desperate attempts to stop. Investigators also found that a special all-weather floor mat installed on the driver's side of the Lexus was slightly larger than a standard Lexus floor mat. One corner of this outsized mat had impinged on the accelerator, trapping it against the car's floor.[4]

In 2009, Toyota enjoyed the highest owner loyalty rankings of any car brand sold in the United States.[5] *Consumer Reports'* 2009 vehicle ratings ranked Toyota vehicles first in five of its ten categories.[6] In the months that followed this horrific, highly publicized crash, however, a different picture of Toyota emerged: one of a company that had often put its own profit motives before the best interests of its customers.

Although Toyota responded to the San Diego accident by announcing the largest recall in its history, critics pointed out that the company had a record of dragging its feet when it came to addressing problems of this kind. The *Los Angeles Times* reported that, dating back as far as 2002, Toyota-made vehicles had been involved in at least a thousand sudden acceleration incidents, more than that of all other car manufacturers *combined*.[7] The newspaper found that at least fifty-six U.S. traffic deaths had been blamed on runaway Toyota vehicles over the years.[8] "[Toyota] knew something was wrong way before that San Diego accident happened," an industry analyst for IHS Global Insight told the *Times*. "That was just the catalyst to get them to finally do something."[9]

Public loss of trust in Toyota led to government distrust. In February 2010, investigators for NHTSA, the National Highway Transportation and Safety Administration, demanded that

Toyota provide the agency with all its engineering reports, internal communications, and customer complaints involving the problem. "That is an unprecedented step for the agency," Ricardo Martinez, a former head of NHTSA in the 1990s, was quoted in one report. "When I was administrator, Toyota was one of the better citizens, but the issues they are dealing with now are very disappointing. They are not acting like the Toyota that built the brand of trust."[10]

Toyota's own internal documents indicated that there had been a change in the company's famous customer-centered culture. Congressional investigators uncovered a Toyota presentation document in which executives claimed to have saved the company hundreds of millions of dollars through regulatory foot-dragging—by negotiating "favorable recall outcomes" with NHTSA.[11] The document showed, among other things, how Toyota had saved $100 million in 2007 by negotiating a limited recall of floor mats in fifty-five thousand Camry and Lexus models under investigation for sudden acceleration. Agreeing to that recall in 2007 helped Toyota avoid further government scrutiny on the issue,[12] and the document labeled these and other regulatory delays and settlements as "Toyota safety wins."[13] NHTSA would end up fining Toyota nearly $70 million for delaying recalls and failing to disclose defects in a timely manner as required by law.[14] The largest previous NHTSA fine levied on any automaker had been $1 million.[15]

The recalls and negative publicity had an inevitable impact on Toyota's bottom line. At the time of the San Diego crash, Toyota ranked number two in car sales in the United States, with a market share of 17 percent. In the first ten months of 2011, that share shrank to just 12.6 percent of the market.[16] The depth of Toyota's loss of credibility was underlined by a public opinion poll taken in January 2010 after the president of Toyota's U.S. division went on the *Today* show to discuss the safety recalls. After reviewing a clip of the Toyota executive's *Today* interview, 56 percent of those surveyed said they were unlikely to buy a Toyota. Only 37 percent had said they were unlikely to buy a Toyota *before* viewing the clip.[17]

There had been a change in leadership at Toyota's Japan headquarters in July 2009, and that gave Toyota the opportunity to make a clean breast of its problems. Akio Toyoda, the new president of Toyota and a grandson of the automaker's founder, flew in from Japan to appear on February 24, 2010, before the House of Representatives' committee on oversight and government reform. Speaking through a translator, Toyoda expressed sorrow for the loss of life in Toyota vehicles and "condolences from the deepest part of my heart." He singled out the Saylor family for special condolences by saying, "I would like to send my prayers again. And I will do everything in my power to ensure that such a tragedy never happens again."

Toyoda went on to concede that his company's great growth in previous years had likely come at the expense of its customers. "Quite frankly," he said, "I fear the pace at which we have grown may have been too quick. I would like to point out here that Toyota's priority has traditionally been the following: first, safety; second, quality; third, volume. These priorities became confused, and we were not able to stop, think and make improvement [sic] as much as we are able to before, and our basic stance to listen to customers' voice, to make better products has weakened somewhat."

He then announced a change in the way Toyota would address safety issues and recalls in the future. A higher layer of management, he said, "will make responsible decisions from the perspective of customer safety first." Previously, Toyoda noted, it had been left to an engineering division in Japan to confirm "whether there are technical problems and make decisions on the necessity of recalls."

"However," he told the committee members, "reflecting on the issues today, what we lacked was the customer perspective."[18]

Who Comes First?

Product recalls and other embarrassments can provide companies with precious moments of truth such as these. The instant a company's products fall under a public cloud, the spotlight turns to the corporate leadership to take a stand and answer the question: Who comes first, people or profits?

When Chris and his academic colleague Nico Kervyn conducted a nationally representative survey of U.S. adults for the *Wall Street Journal* in September 2010 to gauge public reaction to product recalls, the results showed that 93 percent of the public believes that recalls offer "an opportunity for a company or brand to show their true colors, and demonstrate whether they care more about consumers or their own profits." Every company confronted with a serious public image problem has a choice to make. Either it can show its worthy intentions toward its customers, as we hope and expect it will, or it can deflect blame and take a narrower, more immediately self-serving view—which is often the case.

From the perspective of warmth and competence, there is often a mismatch between what we as customers expect to hear from companies in crisis and how executives at most of those companies prefer to respond. Companies engulfed in a scandal, disaster, or product recall often put up proud faces of competence, as if to reassure us that they have the situation under control. But at that moment what we desire most are signals of warmth. If our internal warmth detectors are not satisfied that a troubled company has worthy intentions toward us, then we naturally suspect that its leaders' assertions of competence are aimed at preserving the company's profits first, and our interests second.

The most famous such moment of truth in history was probably the one endured by Johnson & Johnson in 1982, when seven Chicago-area residents died from swallowing Extra-Strength Tylenol capsules that had been poisoned with cyanide. When the company was notified of the poisonings on the morning of September 30, 1982, it immediately canceled advertising for Tylenol and recalled all the capsule versions of Tylenol, at an estimated cost of $100 million. Although the company was quickly found to be blameless in the poisonings, some advertising and marketing experts at the time assumed the Tylenol brand name had been fatally injured by the incident and would never recover. Instead, Johnson and Johnson launched a publicity campaign that put its top executives on national television to reassure the public that the tainted capsules were the work of one deranged individual. When Tylenol capsules returned to stores in early 1983, they were packed in triple-sealed bottles devised by Johnson and Johnson to quell any lingering concerns about product safety. Within a year, Tylenol had regained almost all of its previous market share.[19]

To be sure, when a company is hit with product recalls, it's natural for company leaders to fear that we will judge them harshly for their lack of competence. In the same *Wall Street Journal* survey, a significant minority of the U.S. adults surveyed—43 percent— agreed at least somewhat with this statement: "With today's technology, product defects and safety issues that lead to recalls should be completely avoidable, so companies that issue recalls must be incompetent." Fear of that judgment by the public has motivated many companies to try to keep their mistakes quiet, even if those buried mistakes may blow up on them later.

The trouble with that kind of thinking is that it ignores how forgiving we tend to be of companies who make honest mistakes and then apologize for them. More than 90 percent of those surveyed agreed that "Despite modern technology and honorable intentions, even the best run companies and brands can make mistakes that lead to product recalls." Having been embarrassed by a terrible mistake, the public determination of your competence might rest with your perceived warmth— whether you are judged as having made an error despite good intentions.

A July 2010 warmth and competence study of one thousand U.S. adults by Chris, Susan, and Nico Kervyn revealed that BP, then in the midst of the Deepwater Horizon disaster, was ranked with greater contempt (scoring low in both warmth and competence) than any other brand studied. Only the banks associated with the 2008 financial crisis came close to BP in terms of low regard by the public at large.

Toyota, whose vehicle recalls were earning it almost as much negative publicity as BP, scored well above BP and the banks in the July 2010 study. However, survey respondents still rated Toyota far below average on both warmth and competence, which marked severe erosion in brand reputation for the company, placing it far behind rivals Honda and Ford in both perceptions. Toyota's standing had suffered—albeit not nearly so much as that of BP, Goldman Sachs, and Citibank.

Farther up on the scales of both warmth and competence was the Tylenol brand. Like Toyota, the banks, and BP, Tylenol had been suffering from months of negative news at the time of the survey. Tylenol manufacturer McNeil Consumer Healthcare and its parent company, Johnson & Johnson, voluntarily recalled children's medicines after FDA investigators found irregularities in its manufacturing processes. A toll-free hotline for consumer inquiries was quickly overwhelmed with calls.[20] *Advertising Age* wondered aloud in a headline, "What's Ailing J&J—And Why Isn't Its Rep Hurting?"[21] Johnson & Johnson, singularly among the troubled brands in the *Wall Street Journal* survey, has a long record of responding to trouble by going beyond what is necessary to ensure the safety of its customers.

When "Customer First" Turns Into Company First

For at least seven years, Toyota evaluated sudden acceleration reports on the basis of competence—who was at fault? In nearly all

Figure 6.1. Composite Warmth and Competence Ratings Across Multiple Studies[22]

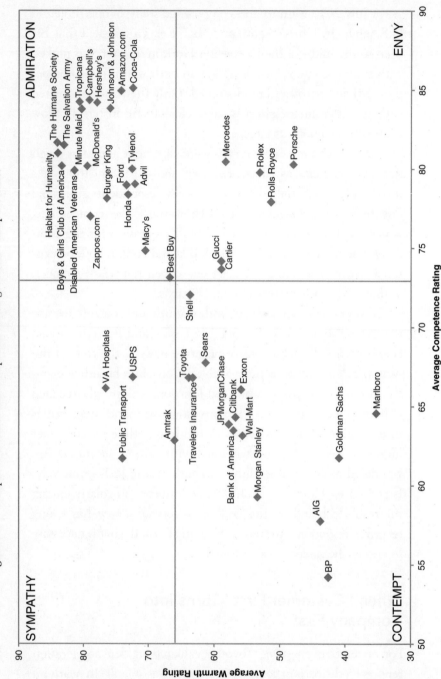

cases, Toyota investigators failed to find any mechanical defects, and therefore determined that "driver error" was to blame in each sudden-acceleration crash.

NHTSA would eventually raise a serious concern about how such a case-by-case approach might not serve the best interests of Toyota customers. NHTSA explained, "We are seeking to determine whether Toyota viewed the underlying defects too narrowly . . . without fully considering the broader issue of sudden acceleration and any associated safety-related defects that warrant recalls." Buried in that bureaucratese is a simple question: If driver errors were killing and injuring Toyota customers, why didn't the company try to help its customers avoid making such dangerous mistakes?

This is another case in which more warmth could have led to more competence within an organization. NHTSA crash investigators noted that Mark Saylor could have saved the lives of everyone in the runaway Lexus if he'd known how to shut off the engine—by holding down the power button for three seconds. Although that information appears buried in the owner's manual, it is not printed on or near the power button itself. Had Toyota engineers looked at the problem from the point of view of a terrified driver with a jammed-open throttle, they might have recommended putting little stickers near the dashboard power buttons that read: "Press and hold for emergency stop."

A second cure for a jammed accelerator had been discovered years ago. Since 2003, many other automakers had added a "brake override" feature to their braking systems. Brake override senses when the accelerator and brake pedals are both depressed, and responds by cutting fuel to the engine. The feature is so simple it can be can be installed with a mere change in the car's software. After the San Diego crash, Toyota agreed to make brake override standard on its new vehicles, but the question remains why it didn't do so years earlier, when the first reports of sudden acceleration came to the attention of Toyota officials. Worthy intentions would have inspired better engineering. Warmth would have increased competence.

Toyota even could have looked to a precedent set by the German car manufacturer Audi. In 1986, Audi was defending itself against its own set of sudden acceleration complaints. Drivers claimed that the automatic transmission on the luxury Audi 5000 model would lurch out of control from a dead stop. By the end of 1986, Audi had received 417 reports of such incidents, with 228 injuries and 4 reported deaths. Speculation at the time was that the problem could pose the greatest damage to a car brand's image since GM was forced to scrap the rollover-plagued Corvair in 1969.[23]

Much like Toyota's engineers, Audi investigators initially found fault with Audi customers. Some drivers, they discovered, were putting their cars into gear with the accelerator depressed, causing their cars to take off suddenly. So Audi tried to educate drivers to keep their foot on the brake before shifting into gear. Insulted and angry drivers sensed a lack of worthy intentions from Audi, and assumed the company was shirking its responsibilities by blaming the victims of its products. They responded by organizing into an Audi Victims Network and started lobbying for a recall.[24]

Only then were Audi engineers inspired to provide a simple engineering solution. A shift-lock mechanism was added to hundreds of thousands of recalled cars, preventing the transmission from being engaged unless the brake pedal is depressed. The complaints dried up, and both Audi sales and the Audi brand image recovered. In 2006, the auto industry agreed to make the shift-lock feature (known as BTSI, or "Betsy") standard in all vehicles, because it prevents an unattended child from putting a car into gear while playing with the shifter.

Toyota's total costs, in terms of lost sales and the cost of recall repairs, were estimated at $2 billion in February 2010.[25] In December 2012, Toyota settled a massive class action lawsuit by agreeing to spend another $1.1 billion to install a brake override function in existing Toyotas and to reimburse Toyota owners for the reduced value of their cars. Car owners who sold their cars between September 1, 2009 (three days after Mark Saylor and his family died in the San Diego crash) and December 31, 2010 are eligible for the program.[26] Toyota has also settled for $10 million with the survivors of Mark Saylor and his passengers. However, so many other sudden acceleration lawsuits are outstanding that some trial lawyers believe their aggregate cost to Toyota will far exceed another $1 billion, bringing total costs to nearly $5 billion.

Toyota could have saved dozens of lives and billions of dollars if, at the earliest reports of sudden acceleration problems, the company had exerted as much effort and creative thinking toward protecting its customers as it did toward protecting its profits. Toyota's priorities had already been evident to anyone who had wrecked a car or been hurt by one of Toyota's jammed accelerators. It took the tragedy in San Diego for those choices to reach public attention and prompt the president of Toyota to come to Washington, DC, to reassert the values that had made the company great.

Forgivable Faults

The biblical book of Proverbs tells us that "Pride goeth before destruction, and an haughty spirit before a fall."[27] Social science tells similar stories about human nature and why those who cling to prideful claims of competence are so much harder to forgive than those who humbly admit their faults. When companies such as Johnson & Johnson and Toyota confess to their failings, we have a spontaneous desire to forgive and forget. In contrast, the defensive utterances by the leadership of BP, Goldman Sachs, and Bank of America during their times of crisis after the Deep Horizon spill and the 2008 economic crash have left us mainly with indelible impressions of their unworthy intentions.

A team of researchers led by Julie Juola Exline at Case Western Reserve University has shown that we avoid extending our forgiveness particularly to those who treat us in ways that are entitled and narcissistic.[28] In a series of experiments, the researchers found that a narcissistic and superior attitude is a stronger predictor of "unforgiveness" than any number of other factors, including offense severity, concessions, and relationship commitment. Lack of warmth and a lack of concern for others, as embodied in the self-centered character traits of narcissism, is the most powerful and most commonly unforgiveable of all transgressions.

On the other hand, as long as we detect worthy intentions in the form of honesty and transparency, we have a tendency to overlook even great lapses in competence, and we reward those expressions of worthy intentions with our loyalty. A famous study of audiotape conversations between patients and primary care physicians showed that physicians who talked longer and laughed more with patients, "indicating warmth and friendliness," were much less likely to be sued for malpractice than doctors who had shorter, more businesslike visits. The researchers wrote, "A warm relationship with the physician may make the patient feel that he or she is a real person in the physician's eyes, rather than a disease. The desire for a connection with the physician is particularly important in long-term relationships, such as a relationship with a primary care physician."[29] Other studies of this kind show that low warmth is a highly predictable indicator of the likelihood that a doctor will be sued, even though malpractice is supposed to involve matters of competence.[30]

Some psychology experiments have shown that a lapse in competence can even make otherwise coldly competent people seem more warm and approachable. One classic study demonstrated that for most people, a competent person of superior accomplishments was considered *more* likeable after accidentally spilling a cup of coffee.[31] Back in 1969, experimenters at the University of Texas made a series of videotapes showing a male undergraduate in a coat and tie being interviewed for the position of student ombudsman, the most responsible student job on campus. Two "competent" tapes were made of the interview. In each, the student being interviewed is holding a cup of coffee as he modestly notes his academic and extracurricular achievements: a 3.8 grade point average, varsity swim team, student government, president of the pre-law association, and a list of other college and high school distinctions. The only difference between the two tapes was that one taped interview concludes without incident, while in the other tape, near the end of the interview, the highly competent applicant clumsily spills his hot cup of coffee on himself.

The second set of tapes was labeled the "incompetent" tapes. The same student was shown interviewing for the student ombudsman position, but with a lackluster resume: a grade point average of 1.9, a failed run at student government, and an unfulfilled plan to join the pre-law association. Of the two "incompetent" tapes, one ended without incident and the other ended with the incompetent applicant spilling his coffee.

More than one hundred student participants were each shown one of these tapes and told they were participating in an experiment evaluating interview techniques. They were asked to rate the videotaped job applicant on eight criteria, including how much they liked the applicant, how much they would like to spend a lot of time with applicant, and how much they would like to work with the applicant.

Most students who saw the highly competent applicant spill his coffee found him significantly more likeable than the students who saw the same competent applicant's interview conclude without a coffee spill. For the incompetent applicant, however, the coffee hardly mattered. Most students didn't rank him high for likeability whether he spilled the coffee or not. The conclusion drawn by the researchers was that for most people of average self-esteem, "The superior individual who blunders may be perceived as being closer and more similar to the average subject, and hence more attractive. Average subjects may see the [coffee-spilling] superior as being more approachable."[32]

Because we respond to brands and companies the way we respond to people, it only stands to reason that highly competent brands and companies who suffer from lapses in judgment can emerge from the experience as more "human" and more approachable. Success, it's been said, is determined not by whether you fall down but by how you get up. To that extent, every company's mistake or public embarrassment represents an opportunity to improve its standing in terms of warmth and competence among its customers, but only if the company is ready to respond to its moment of truth with worthy intentions.

Apple's Lost Directions

One highly competent company that figuratively spilled the coffee was Apple, with its launch of the ill-fated Maps app for iPhone in September 2012. One week after releasing the new navigational aid, Apple CEO Tim Cook issued a statement admitting that Apple "fell short" on its commitment to world-class products. "We are extremely sorry for the frustration this has caused our customers," he wrote, "and we are doing everything we can to make Maps better."[33]

Apple's Map app was a major misstep on arrival. It mislabeled geographical features, responded to local search requests with locations thousands of miles away, and failed to offer transit directions. Several drivers using the app to find the Australian town of Mildura almost died when they were directed forty miles off course into a remote desert wilderness. An analysis of fifty thousand random tweets mentioning iPhone Maps found that 22 percent expressed hatred of the app, and another 30 percent expressed ridicule.

The worst thing about iPhone Maps was that it replaced something that had been working just fine. Google Maps had been the default navigation aid on the iPhone since it had launched. Now iPhone users who upgraded their software found that the Google Maps they'd long relied on had been replaced by Apple's home-grown lemon. Mobile industry website BGR.com speculated that Apple likely replaced Google Maps as a logical outgrowth of an ongoing battle between Apple and Google, but "regardless, users are being punished. Thermonuclear war or not, there's no excuse for punishing users."[34]

Cook had been caught putting his company's strategic desires ahead of Apple customers' needs, though he never owned up to that specifically. Instead, in his apology, he did something that maybe no other Apple CEO had ever done before. He acknowledged that other companies might offer something better. "While we're improving Maps," he wrote, iPhone owners might want to try out rival mapping apps and sites by Microsoft, MapQuest, Google, and Nokia.

Did it work? Not really. Although issuing a quick apology and recommending other alternatives was definitely a step in the direction of customers' best interests, it fell short of a complete and transparent explanation of what had happened and why. This absence of transparency and full disclosure doesn't constitute authentic remorse. Cook failed to explain what their intentions had been in rolling out Apple maps or what had gone wrong. He also failed to make a commitment to do whatever it takes to remedy the situation right away or rollback the Apple Maps app in a subsequent software update. In subsequent weeks, it was revealed that Apple knew Maps was in bad shape long before it launched. The CNET.com tech news site reported that software developers who had been given prerelease beta versions of iPhone Maps in June had tried to warn Apple that the app wasn't ready for its debut. "They vented on message boards only other developers and Apple could see," CNET reported.

Before the year was up, Cook had fired two of the senior Apple executives responsible for the Maps fiasco and had stated on national television, "Well, we screwed up. And we are putting the weight of the company behind correcting it."[35] Perhaps that is true, but one thing is for sure: Apple missed a major opportunity to show its customers and the world that it cared more about the needs and safety of its customers than about competing with Google. Unfortunately, they got this one only half right, and that's not enough to demonstrate worthy intentions. It may be a long time before they get another opportunity of the same magnitude to get it completely right.

A Reservoir of Good Will

Highly admired companies, such as Apple, Toyota, and Johnson & Johnson, generally discover that their long records of warmth and competence are very helpful in seeing them through difficult times when they have made serious errors. In Chris's previously mentioned studies of Tylenol's resilient reputation with customers (and that of its parent company, Johnson & Johnson), the results suggest that both Tylenol and Johnson & Johnson had a built up such a large reservoir of goodwill over the years that a series of missteps in its manufacturing processes had failed to shake public faith in the brand or company.

Between January and July 2010, two hundred million bottles of suspect Tylenol, Motrin IB, Rolaids, Benedryl, Zyrtec, and St. Joseph's aspirin were subject to a series of eight separate recalls. The reasons for the recalls cited by the FDA included mysterious musty odors in the packaging, unsanitary manufacturing conditions, and trace amounts of bacteria found on the outside of drums of raw materials used to make the products.[36]

In April 2010, Johnson & Johnson's McNeil division, which makes these over-the-counter medications, decided to shut down a Pennsylvania manufacturing facility indefinitely after the FDA issued a highly critical report on quality control and sanitary conditions at the plant. The shutdown resulted in an almost total removal of many of recalled products from store shelves for more than a year. All Tylenol advertising and promotions were suspended, as well.

Presented with these details, 88 percent of U.S. adults say they believe McNeil has handled the recalls honestly and responsibly. They overwhelmingly believed that Tylenol's decision to suspend advertising and promotions was the right thing to do, and they thought McNeil would be justified in claiming credit for handling the problem honestly and responsibly.

However, Chris's warmth-and-competence research on the recalls showed that both a vast reservoir of goodwill built up over years of Tylenol usage and the company's handling of previous recalls were responsible for customers' unshaken loyalty and purchase intent for the brand. From a warmth and competence point of view, customers who use Tylenol feel they have a relationship with the brand and the people behind it. After years of being satisfied customers, particularly of a product as intimate as a pain reliever, it's against human nature to abandon the product at the first signs of trouble. Our research showed evidence that the 2010 product quality issues, though disconcerting, were interpreted by Tylenol users as a short-term lapse in competence, rather than a signal of unworthy intentions and a lack of warmth toward its loyal customers.

While Tylenol's production challenges and the negative scrutiny they created were certainly nothing for Johnson & Johnson to promote, they responded to their crisis very differently than did Toyota. Despite some early foot dragging, the company ultimately defused the tempest completely by recalling all of its products and shutting the only plant in North America that made them. Wall Street analysts estimates that this move cost the McNeil division nearly $600 million in revenue in 2010 alone. But as a result, the Tylenol brand secured something much more valuable—the unwavering loyalty and purchase intent of its customers. This, and the handling of previous Tylenol recalls, can perhaps be attributed in part to the famous Johnson & Johnson credo, written in 1943, which includes the following:

> Our first responsibility is to the doctors, nurses and patients, to mothers and fathers and all others who use our products and services. In meeting their needs, everything we do must be of high quality . . . Our final responsibility is to shareholders. Business must make a sound profit. We must experiment with new ideas. Research must be carried on, innovative programs developed and mistakes paid for. New equipment must be purchased, new facilities provided and new products launched. Reserves must be created to provide for adverse times. When we operate according to these principles, the stockholders should realize a fair return.[37]

It is precisely this operating philosophy that guided Tylenol through its tampering crisis in the 1980s and allowed it to build up the reservoir of goodwill and trust that buffered it from more serious loyalty damage in 2010. Ironically, other divisions of Johnson & Johnson seem to be burning up goodwill at a furious pace, handling product defects and recalls disastrously. The company's DePuy Synthes medical device division, for instance, faced thousands of lawsuits from patients for knowingly selling faulty hip implants from 2008 to 2010. As with Toyota, poor "moment of truth" decisions like these invariably cost far more in lost sales and reputation damage than doing the right thing up front would have.

Ample evidence shows that a reputation for warmth and competence will draw us to such companies and brands in a way that we will tend to be more trusting and forgiving of their mistakes. For such faults to be forgivable, the brands and companies we've come to trust need to take such setbacks as challenges and moments of truth, in which they seek to cement their relationships by doing what's in our immediate best interest, even if at the temporary expense of their own. It is this kind of loyalty to us that prompts us to reciprocate with loyalty of our own.

The Silver Lining

Researchers who have studied the psychology of "interpersonal forgiving" say that forgiveness represents a change in motivation toward an offending actor. In the act of forgiving, we decrease our motivations to retaliate or estrange ourselves, and we are motivated instead by conciliation and goodwill. One influential social psychology experiment shows that we are apt to forgive when we are able to feel empathy for the offending partner.[38]

Close relationships provide three potential reasons to feel empathy for someone who has hurt you. First, you might feel empathy out of caring about your partner's feelings of guilt and distress for having done something wrong. Second, you might feel empathy out of caring about the partner's feelings of loneliness and isolation because of the strained relationship. Finally, and most directly, feelings of empathy simply may stir in you a yearning to restore positive contact.[39]

Patrick Doyle, the CEO of Domino's, went on national television to say that his pizza hadn't been very good for a while, and he was doing something about it. It's doubtful any of us worried about Doyle's feelings of guilt or loneliness from serving bad pizza and losing customers. But it's not so far-fetched that the humbleness of his apology did indeed arouse feelings of empathy for him and his company. To go and try the new pizza would have an added dimension of emotion: that it would be nice to give the guy another chance.

We humanize companies that mess up, as long as they show us their good intentions. When nearly nine out of ten adults say they feel more loyalty toward a company that handles a product recall responsibly, those results make clear that the public is much more forgiving than most corporate leaders would assume.

The evidence seems to be that every problem we experience in a relationship, no matter how big or small, represents an opportunity to make the relationship stronger if we are able to show worthy intentions that convey both warmth and competence. Companies that are able to come clean about their errors and state their intentions for doing better in the future might actually bring us closer to them than if they had never slipped up in the first place.

The Cable Guy

Sometimes an unsatisfactory customer experience can help build a relationship that actually improves brand loyalty. In 2009, after years of spotty service from Comcast at Chris's house in the Philadelphia area, he decided to switch over to FiOS, Verizon's high-speed fiber optic network. Verizon's customer service representative offered a good price, faster internet speeds, and, importantly, Verizon assured him that he could keep his phone numbers. Chris was working from home frequently at the time, and not having to notify colleagues of new numbers for his business and fax lines was important to him.

Once the new lines were connected to the house's internal phone wiring, the installers pronounced the job complete and left. The next day, Chris received a call from a coworker advising him that a fax hadn't gone through. Chris checked the line and discovered it wasn't responding when he dialed the number. For the next three days, Chris made a series of calls to Verizon's call center in an attempt to sort out the problem. Sometimes he was forced to wait on hold for forty-five minutes or longer during the middle of the day, without making any progress. Verizon representatives tried to persuade Chris that his old fax line number was now lost and irretrievable. But Chris wouldn't take no for an answer. He wanted to keep his number. So they sent another technician to his house.

When Verizon installer Andrew Parkinson showed up the next day, Chris was obviously frustrated. Andrew apologized for the problem Verizon had caused and said he would do everything he could to get the old fax number reinstated. "I'll take care of you," Andrew told him. "I will personally make sure this gets done." Andrew gave Chris his personal cell phone number. He told Chris to call in yet another service order, but to ask for the order number. "When you get your order number," Andrew said, "text it to me, and I'll make sure I'm the one assigned to come out."

Chris followed Andrew's instructions, and Andrew arrived the next day. Regaining a lost or inoperative number required Andrew to contact a series of business offices, repair offices, and network test centers in order to locate the source of the problem. Verizon call center personnel were never able to make such a dedicated effort on Chris's behalf because, as Andrew explained, field worker calls get special treatment. As long as he was calling from a customer's house, or even sitting in a truck in the driveway, his calls to all these offices would be given priority handling. By the end of the day, he'd detected the source of the problem, and the fax line was restored.

Andrew told Chris that it's not company policy for installers to share their phone numbers but that he gives out his number once or twice a week when it's clear that resolving the issue requires a personal touch. "The company expects us to solve a problem as quickly as possible," he explained. "It's a lot easier for me to get a handle on it because I can access more company directories and departments than you can by calling the business office. But if you don't have my information, you're going to have to go back to calling the business office. It's going to get unpleasant, because you'll be starting the process over multiple times."

From Chris's perspective, Andrew was the first Verizon employee he'd encountered who showed him any worthy intentions. Andrew demonstrated high levels of both warmth and competence, in that he cared about Chris's best interests and obviously took pleasure in solving problems on Chris's behalf. Chris's only disappointment was Andrew couldn't accept a tip as a token of his gratitude.

"I work with plenty of guys who have empathy for customers," Andrew told Chris. "For us it's much more satisfying to help people than to knock on their door, tell them we can't really help, have a great day, and leave." It turned out that Andrew was Verizon's go-to guy in the area, the fixer. When a chronic complaint comes down from the area vice-president's office, supervisors give Andrew the assignment.

Chris made sure to keep Andrew's personal number handy. A year later, when Chris wanted to extend FiOS service to his basement, he figured, "Hey, I have a guy inside Verizon." Andrew came out and put his skills to work, seamlessly threading CAT-5 cable up through the walls and attic of the house and then down into the basement so that Chris's teenage sons could operate their Xbox from the lower level.

Now when Comcast sends mail and even door-to-door solicitations urging Chris to come back, he has to laugh, because although he's not sure he feels loyalty toward Verizon, he knows for sure that he has unwavering loyalty to Andrew Parkinson. Comcast may offer any number of advantages over Verizon, but unless they can offer someone like Andrew, Chris isn't interested in changing services. Andrew is Verizon's secret loyalty advantage. So secret, in fact, that not even Verizon recognizes the remarkable impact he has on customer loyalty.

Learning from Mistakes

The prospect of forgiveness, the hope of being returned to former glory, motivates troubled companies to do better. Both Toyota and Johnson & Johnson have since emerged from their embarrassing series of recalls as stronger, improved companies in many respects. Despite topping the automotive recall list in the

United States for three years running, Toyota ended 2012 with a 13.5 percent increase in sales for the final quarter, which beat the industry average in sales growth. Even with the $1.1 billion settlement costs associated with the recalls, Toyota's income for 2012 reached a five-year high, indicating a complete return to the company's conditions prior to the recalls.

"A crisis can help you sort through your priorities," writes Jeffrey K. Liker in *Toyota Under Fire*. Liker points out how Toyota's recall crisis illuminated "cultural breakdowns, communication inefficiencies, and creeping bureaucracy" that had inhibited Toyota's famous customer focus during a period of rapid growth.[40] The recalls created such a shock to Toyota's reputation and revenues that the new president of the company was able to right the ship with the help of Toyota's strong underlying culture.

Johnson & Johnson entered 2013 with a leadership transition under way. The company's sales for 2012 were "solid," according to the new CEO, Alex Gorsky, but he cut scheduled year-end bonuses by 5 percent to indicate to employees that "solid" was no longer good enough. With the FDA and McNeil acting under a consent decree signed in 2011, the FDA's expanded oversight over three McNeil manufacturing plants actually lends credibility to McNeil's efforts to restore its reputation.

Based on everything that company officials have learned from their problems, Johnson & Johnson is now markedly more cautious and proactive about recalls. On February 17, 2012, the company announced a recall of 574,000 bottles of Infants' Tylenol, simply because it had received a total of seventeen customer complaints that a new dosing system built into the packaging wasn't working correctly.[41] Setbacks of any kind should be embraced as opportunities for companies to demonstrate how customers really are their top priority—because authentic chances of that kind don't come up in the normal course of business.

In the Relationship Renaissance, everything moves faster, mistakes will keep happening, and we are all poised to watch how companies react when they do. The choices companies make under such circumstances will determine how long it takes for customers to forgive and forget. If companies can come clean early and transparently, their customers may reward them with the empathy and forgiveness characteristic of close relationships. And our relationships with companies and brands, or lack thereof, are getting more important by the day.

Chapter Seven

The Relationship Renaissance

Navigating the road ahead

The question this book should raise is not whether business people are warm and competent, but whether they're perceived that way. Even if they think they've expressed worthy intentions to others who are important to them, can they be sure they're experienced as such? And if they learned that they weren't, what would they be willing to do about it?

Most company and brand executives, after all, believe they are acting reasonably and prudently when they make critical business decisions. Like most people, they view themselves as being both warm and competent, and they expect others to view them as such. They are largely unaware of how their decisions and resulting actions will be perceived by their customers and other stakeholders.

For all of us, ensuring that our warmth and competence, our worthy intentions, are getting through to others reduces to three imperative actions. We first must overcome our natural inability to fully appreciate how we come across to others, by soliciting honest feedback from them. Second, we must embrace that feedback and significantly change our words and actions, just as surely as Dan Hesse did at Sprint and Patrick Doyle did at Domino's. And finally, we must fundamentally shift our priorities. Responding to candid feedback won't accomplish much if we, as customers or companies, remain focused only on our own best interests. That's the promise of understanding the principles of warmth and competence—they encourage us all to be better people.

Imperative 1: Become More Self-Aware

As sophisticated as we are at instantly judging the intentions and abilities of others, we all suffer from dangerous blind spots that hinder our ability to fully understand how we are perceived. In this digital, mobile, and networked world, when it has never been easier to make thousands or even millions of impressions on others, it's accordingly never been more important to be aware of how our words and actions are perceived by others in terms of warmth and competence. Ongoing self-awareness of this kind may well be the most crucial competency we all must develop in the Relationship Renaissance.

Companies and brands that genuinely desire the trust and loyalty of their customers need to commit to measuring and managing perceptions of their warmth and competence as diligently as they assess and manage their finances. These two measurable dimensions of human perception, as developed and refined through collaborative research, provide the means for all of us to diagnose whether we are succeeding in communicating our worthy intentions to others. We can use these dimensions to help us see through our blind spots and adjust our behavior accordingly.

The most basic dimensions of warmth are simply whether others see us as warm and trustworthy. Similarly, the most basic dimensions of competence assess the degree to which others see us as competent and capable. These are not difficult questions for us to ask others for feedback on, though it may be socially awkward for them to provide candid feedback on them to us directly.

Take the Loyalty Test

Soliciting direct feedback—and receiving it directly—can be awkward. To help facilitate this process, we've created a free and simple tool at www.LoyaltyTest.com. There you can quickly and easily solicit anonymous feedback on how customers perceive a particular company or brand from a warmth and competence perspective. The resulting feedback will offer you a basic demonstration of these principles and some insight into the level of trust and loyalty others feel toward that organization. You may be surprised by what you learn from the Loyalty Test, just as officials at Coca-Cola, Hershey's, and McNeil were surprised after more comprehensive studies were performed on their behalf. But once having taken the test, you'll better understand the changes that organization will need to make to reliably earn the trust and loyalty of customers.

Gathering this kind of feedback—on a company or brand—is in no way a new strain of psychological manipulation, reminiscent of the "hidden persuaders" and "subliminal seduction" of yesteryear or of today's "emotional branding" strategies. The principle of worthy intentions requires companies to forge genuine relationships with their customers, and genuine relationships cannot be measured as reward points issued, the number of calls handled by a call center, or customer "touches" recorded in CRM software programs.

As described in Chapter Four, those disruptive technologies can alienate other people just as easily as they can engage them. Applied one way, technologies can bring us much closer than ever to the people who sell to us. Applied differently, the same technologies can entirely eliminate the warmth and humanity from our economic exchanges.

The phenomenon of big data is a case in point. Huge amounts of personal information about virtually every consumer can now be mined with increasingly sophisticated software in order to detect subtle buying patterns far beyond what was possible just a few decades ago. But the amount of information now available for mining is almost incalculable, and it includes not just easily digested data points, such as demographic information and products purchased, but also the richer and more complex information contained in the pictures we post on Facebook, the subjects discussed in our emails, and just about anything we leave in the wake of our passage through the day.

Such information can provide marketers with valuable insights, but it can also be intrusive and disaffecting. Big-box retailer Target, for instance, has taken data mining to a new level of sophistication. The *New York Times Magazine* revealed in February 2012 that Target had figured out how to predict its customers' pregnancies.[1] The company's marketing analytics experts were able to identify twenty-five products that could be analyzed along with individual customer data to produce a "pregnancy prediction score" for female shoppers. The scoring analysis estimates due dates with surprising accuracy, enabling Target to send out coupons timed to each stage of an individual customer's presumed pregnancy.

Such quantitative research represents an attempt to get to "know" customers in a way that's scalable and actionable. But, like so much else that companies do today, the methodology ultimately devalues human contact and trust. One day an irate father stormed into a Target store and demanded to know why his teenage daughter was receiving coupons for motherhood-related items: was the company encouraging her to get pregnant? Target responded by disguising its expectant mother strategy in subsequent mailings, judiciously mixing in ads and coupons for products unrelated to parenthood. Chastened for overreaching, Target tried to make it harder for pregnant women to know if they're being "Targeted."

We see the same level of data-mining sophistication in the way Google uses Gmail members' email content and search engine history to send ads their way. Such practices may exhibit a certain level of technical competence, but these tactics lack the warmth that our research has shown will determine customer loyalty and build relationships. Inevitably, this kind of exploitive technical "competence" will prove incompetent in producing actual financial success for those who exercise it. We are bound to grow weary of being manipulated in these ways, and we will naturally gravitate toward companies that resist using technology for exploitive purposes and use it instead to express their worthy intentions and establish authentic relationships.

Microsoft, for example, has tried to make a virtue of the fact that it doesn't data mine email content in its webmail service, Outlook.com. In 2013, the company launched ads aimed directly at Google's data mining practices. "You're Getting Scroogled" screamed the headline of one such ad in the *Wall Street Journal*.[2] The ad directs readers to Scroogled.com, where they can sign up for Microsoft's Outlook.com and sign a petition to tell "Google to stop going through personal email." By framing its advertising campaign as though it were a social movement, Microsoft was attempting to appeal to those Gmail users turned off by the invasion of their privacy for the purpose of commerce.

Google's and Target's data mining are just a few ways in which powerful new technologies remain mired in the Middle Ages of Marketing paradigm. The problem is that the micro segmentation, tracking cookies, and retargeted ads and content that characterize big data and search engine optimization accomplish little in the way of getting to know customers by name and building meaningful relationships with them. That's part of why we find the intrusions on privacy they often involve so creepy.

The nature of both human relationships as well at those with companies and brands is such that candid and objective feedback is not usually provided in any timely or consistent way. For us to truly know where we stand and to become more mindful of when we act in the future, this feedback must instead be actively sought and gathered. The first step in building self-awareness is to ask for candid feedback and then listen with an open mind and genuine interest.

Imperative 2: Embrace Significant Change

As Domino's, Sprint, and others have shown, companies can thrive by listening to their customers—including their most spirited critics—and using what they learn to revolutionize their approach to what they do. That's how Domino's turned around its pizza offerings. That's how Sprint went from worst to first in customer service. Domino's in particular shows how we can raise our expectations for relationships with companies that are important to us.

We now expect to be able to communicate with companies, and we expect them to listen. That two-way communication is the basis of any relationship, whether it be with people, brands, or even companies. We naturally want relationships only with those who approach us with worthy intentions. Those in charge of companies and brands must be willing to thoroughly examine their priorities, policies, and practices from a warmth and competence perspective. For relationships to work in the Relationship Renaissance, the people behind the brands must genuinely want to be better people and act accordingly, with worthy intentions.

As we perceive improved behavior from companies that are important to us, we will in turn reward them with our loyalty, treat them as if they *are* better people, and so on in a virtuous circle. Psychologists call this the "Michelangelo phenomenon."[3] The more we behave toward relationship partners as if they have achieved their ideal selves, the more likely they are to attain those ideal selves. In this way, we "sculpt" the idealized selves of our relationship partners, just as Michelangelo's imagination caused an idealized figure to emerge from a slab of marble. But, as researchers point out, the partner in such a relationship must actually aspire to the ideal self we are assuming and affirming in our interactions with that partner.

We see the Michelangelo phenomenon in the wake of the corporate missteps and product recalls discussed in Chapter Six. Companies that behave honestly, transparently, and unselfishly after such mishaps demonstrate an ideal to which they aspire, though they may have fallen short in a particular instance. We customers forgave the company's leadership, and in forgiving them, we affirm their ideal, encouraging them to continue to aspire to it. Similarly, company executives who welcome criticism and respond wholeheartedly to customer dissatisfaction demonstrate their desire to be better. Even the harshest critics, when treated fairly and with respect, often become a company's most loyal fans, because in getting their complaints resolved they've been granted a sense of that company's ideal self.

Does that sound unrealistic? Consider how McDonald's has changed its approach to criticism over the years. Back in 1986, McDonald's was challenged by a small group of British environmental activists distributing a pamphlet titled "What's wrong with McDonald's: Everything they don't want you to know." It alleged that the company sold unhealthy food, exploited children through its advertising, mistreated its workers, and destroyed vast tracts of rainforest for paper, among other transgressions.

McDonald's reacted to this obscure organization's little campaign by hiring informers to infiltrate the group, suing two group members for libel, and threatening to sue news outlets reporting on the group's accusations.[4] The "McLibel" case, as the legal action came to be known, dragged along for more than ten years, and although the defendants ultimately lost in the British courts, they won significant victories in the court of global public opinion. The Internet became a powerful platform for their supporters, exposing McDonald's to withering scorn far beyond the British Isles. That little "What's Wrong with McDonald's" pamphlet was translated into twenty-seven languages and still lives online.[5] McDonald's extreme defensive actions backfired, fueling an attack that might have died out quietly on its own.

Today McDonald's responds to criticism much differently. Consistent with the Michelangelo phenomenon, McDonald's has been sculpted to some extent by its critics. Following the 2004 independent documentary *Super Size Me*, which charged McDonald's with contributing to the U.S. epidemic of obesity, the company eventually phased out its popular super-sized meal option. Since then, McDonald's has sought more environmentally friendly suppliers, eliminated trans fats from its French fries, added apple slices to Happy Meals, and included other healthier choices on its menu. Whatever can be said of McDonald's shortcomings today, the company does not attempt to crush its opposition as it once did.

For customers and companies, today's Relationship Renaissance can be a two-way street, just as in preindustrial commerce when the artisan derived as much satisfaction from producing a choice piece of craftsmanship as the patron did in purchasing it. But in order to fully embrace the value of warmth, competence, and loyalty insights, companies and brands must shift from a mentality of control, defensiveness, and unresponsiveness to one that is more open to understanding how they are perceived and to greater willingness to respond and adapt accordingly.

This will require a comprehensive reevaluation of the policies, practices, and processes that companies and brands use to conduct business every day, with emphasis on understanding what they convey and demonstrate from a warmth and competence perspective. Simply trying to adjust the messaging in marketing campaigns or corporate social responsibility efforts will have little effect, and it could actually do further harm if they are perceived to be disingenuous.

The reason for this is that when marketing and corporate social responsibility efforts are made in ways that are warm, competent, and consistent with the principle of worthy intentions, they give us valuable insights into the intentions and abilities of the people leading that organization. When they are conducted in ways that clearly involve a quid pro quo, like so many "we'll make a donation if you make a purchase" campaigns, we see through them as largely self-serving sales promotions. In contrast, it's those genuinely selfless acts by companies and brands in the best interests of others that provide us with meaningful insight on their true intentions and abilities. This is what we respond to with trust, admiration, and loyalty.

Many of the companies and brands that best align their efforts with our warmth and competence expectations—like Honest Tea, Lululemon, Zappos, and Chobani—began doing so from their very inception, guided by a purpose-based mission that became woven into the fabric of how they do business each day. Companies and brands that have made a good living during the Middle Ages of Marketing paradigm face a much more difficult challenge, because fundamentally changing the way they do business will not be easy. However, those hoping to grow and thrive during the Relationship Renaissance need to embrace this new form of "enlightened self-interest" and adapt accordingly. The alternative is likely a future filled with cold, faceless commerce; transient customers; unfulfilled employees; and thin profit margins

Imperative 3: Fundamentally Shift Priorities

Ultimately, it's not enough to respond and change selectively in response to candid feedback from others. Lasting change requires a sincere examination and adjustment of the goals and priorities that led us astray in the first place. Sustained success in the future will require companies and brands to significantly shift their emphasis from an excessive focus on short-term shareholder value to a much more balanced approach that creates shared value for multiple stakeholders, with particular emphasis on customers and the employees who serve them.

Shifting this emphasis will not be easy, especially for publicly traded companies that have a long tradition of focus on quarterly returns. More recently, the age-old constraint of maximizing shareholder value has been intensified by an obsession with short-term profits, leading companies to manage from quarter to quarter and live in fear of meeting the almost imaginary number provided in earnings advisory calls with Wall Street analysts.

Some would have us believe this has always been the case, but that is not so. According to Peter Drucker, the professional managers of the 1930s and 1940s saw their mission as balancing the short term with the long term.[6] In fact, the 1950s saw much discussion, led in part by Drucker, of management's obligation to balance the interests of what have since come to be called "stakeholders": shareholders, employees, suppliers, communities, and others who have an interest in the company's success. That balance was lost, Drucker says, during the takeover wars of the 1980s, when corporate raiders were backed by institutional investors legally obligated to support the raiders if the sale of a company offered even a slightly greater return. In the unrelenting pursuit of short-term profit maximization, shareholder interests seem to have obscured the long-held belief that the way to maximize long-term shareholder value was by putting the best interests of customers first, as evidenced by the J&J credo and other similar time-honored management principles.

Mark Kramer and Michael Porter—the latter the originator of the concept of "competitive advantage," one of the most influential business concepts in recent history—have called for corporations to move from simply creating shareholder value to creating "shared value." In 2006, they argued that if "corporations were to analyze their prospects for social responsibility using the same frameworks that guide their core business choices, they would discover that [corporate social responsibility] can be much more than a cost, a constraint, or a charitable deed—it can be a source of opportunity, innovation, and competitive advantage."[7]

One of the first companies to embrace such an outlook was PepsiCo, the owner of such well-known brands as Pepsi-Cola, Tropicana, Quaker Oats, Gatorade, and Frito-Lay. PepsiCo's experience shows evidence of the difficulties that publicly owned companies face in pursuing a path guided by worthy intentions.

In 2006, under the leadership of CEO Indra Nooyi, the company launched an ambitious makeover it called "Performance with Purpose." The goal, wrote Nooyi in that year's annual report, is to achieve "the balance between providing you with solid returns on your investments and working to create a defining corporation for the new millennium—one that strives to *do better by doing better*."[8]

By 2006, PepsiCo's main business categories had been under siege for some time. Sugary drinks and salty snacks—the mainstays of PepsiCo's revenues—were widely seen as contributing the epidemic of obesity in the United States, much like McDonald's offerings. Rates of diabetes, hypertension, heart disease, stroke, and other diet-related conditions all were increasing. The World Health Organization had recommended increased consumption of fruits and vegetables, the removal of trans fats from food, and reduced intake of saturated fats, sugar, and salt. Governments in the United States and abroad were considering "fat taxes" on the industry's products. Investors worried that, like Big Tobacco in the 1980s, the snack food industry would be vulnerable to costly lawsuits alleging that its products contributed to public health problems. JPMorgan Chase ranked PepsiCo fourth among food and beverage companies most at risk for such lawsuits.[9] Meanwhile, consumers were voting with their wallets, and sugary drinks were in the midst of a long decline in beverage market share.

Against this backdrop, PepsiCo promised to deliver performance by striving to "increase revenues, market share, volume, profits and earnings per share, while reducing costs and improving productivity."[10] At the same time, they acknowledged that "today's consumers increasingly view their spending decisions as a way to make a difference in the world . . . [and] want to see their values reflected in the products they buy and their communities strengthened by the businesses they support." The company vowed to meet those needs in three ways: by expanding its portfolio of healthier food and beverage products, by reducing the company's environmental impact in its water packaging and energy use, and by creating a company culture of equality, diversity, and inclusion.

Nooyi hired a former World Health Organization executive director to run the company's Global Health Policy. In 2010, the company created a Global Nutrition Group to continue a decade-old effort to enlarge its portfolio of healthy products. The goal: grow what the company called its "Good-for-You" products from a $10 billion business to a $30 billion business by 2020. They resolved to get there by building on existing brands like Gatorade, Tropicana, and Quaker Oats and by acquiring and developing other healthy products. The company also worked to improve the nutritional profiles of its core products, reduced its advertising to children, and participated in an industry-wide initiative to remove full-calorie soft drinks from schools in the United States.

In a detailed case study of the Performance with Purpose initiative, a team of Harvard Business School professors concluded that PepsiCo's leadership clearly saw Performance with Purpose as more than just a strategy for long-term financial growth: "It was also a vision of good global citizenship."[11] The case study credited Nooyi with understanding that her company has "a soul . . . made up of all the people who comprise the enterprise."[12]

But five years into the program, after the flagship Pepsi-Cola brand fell to number three behind Coke and Diet Coke in U.S. soft drink rankings, PepsiCo began to run into familiar pressures facing large, publicly traded companies: the clamor from shareholders to produce earnings, not earnestness. An investment group led by activist shareholder Ralph Whitworth took a $600-million stake in the company with a goal of trying to force it to spin off its slow-growing beverage unit into a separate business. Analysts, too, suggested that splitting PepsiCo's beverage and snacks divisions into separate companies would create more shareholder value, just as Kraft had recently done with its snacks and grocery businesses.

Some observers questioned whether PepsiCo's emphasis on healthier products had come at the expense of overall growth and shareholder returns. In 2011 the phrase "Performance with Purpose" was missing from the annual report for the first time since 2006 (it would reappear in the 2012 report.) In February 2012, PepsiCo slashed 8,700 jobs, reorganized its business units, and announced aggressive new marketing plans for its core products. The PepsiCo board said it was standing by Nooyi, her team, and their strategy, but stressed that directors were "committed to maximizing shareholder value."

Rick Wartzman of the Drucker Institute wrote at the time that Nooyi "demonstrates, as much as any CEO I know of, how immensely difficult it can be to pursue such noble ends—especially at a time when 'maximizing shareholder value' remains a mantra among many."[13] In a system that stresses raising short-term stock prices to the exclusion of all other considerations, "doing better by doing good" is next to impossible. Many observers trace the primacy of shareholder value back to a nearly century-old decision of the Michigan Supreme Court in the textbook case of Ford v. Dodge. Said the court: "A business corporation is organized and carried on primarily for the profit of the stockholders. The powers of the directors are to be employed for that end. The discretion of directors is to be exercised in the choice of means to attain that end, and does not extend to a change in the end itself, to the reduction of profits, or to the non-distribution of profits among stockholders in order to devote them to other purposes."[14]

Thirty-one states do have what are called "constituency" laws that allow—but do not require—directors to consider constituents other than shareholders when making decisions. Delaware, however, is not one of them, and Delaware is the legal home to

50 percent of all U.S. publicly traded companies and 63 percent of the Fortune 500. Most other state courts take Delaware law into account when interpreting their own corporate laws.[15] Even in states with constituency laws, the general fiduciary duty of directors continues to be maximizing shareholder value.

In 2011, at just about the time Nooyi was encountering headwinds from analysts and shareholders, Porter and Kramer weighed in with some specific steps that companies could take to create shared value. They advocated for companies to reconceive their products and markets, redefine productivity in the value chain, and build supportive industry clusters at company locations, all with the goal of benefiting multiple stakeholders in a virtuous circle of mutual support.[16] They cited the efforts of such giants as GE, Wal-Mart, Nestlé, Johnson & Johnson, and Unilever to create shared value of this kind. Nestlé, for example, redesigned its coffee procurement processes, provided advice to small growers, helped them secure resources, and began paying them directly for higher-quality beans. Higher yields and better beans raised the farmers' incomes and provided Nestlé and its customers with a reliable supply of good coffee.

Patagonia, the outdoor clothing and gear manufacturer, took a similar path after learning that the poisonous chemicals used in the conventional growing of cotton made this so-called "natural" fiber what the company called "by far the greatest environmental evildoer" of all the fabrics they were using. Patagonia then made a difficult decision, based entirely on its worthy intentions. In the fall of 1994, Patagonia committed to making all of their cotton sportswear from 100-percent organic cotton by 1996—a switch of sixty-six products within just eighteen months. At the time, it was an ambitious commitment, since there were no large commercial U.S. growers of organic cotton. But the commitment created a national market for organic cotton, just as Nestlé's commitment to farmers created a market for high-quality coffee beans. Patagonia managed to make its deadline, and its cotton products have been made with all-organic cotton ever since.

What can companies learn from examples such as PepsiCo's, Nestlé's, and Patagonia's? Will investors preoccupied with short-term results continue to challenge company efforts to rebalance their priorities, as they did at PepsiCo? Or will we evolve a system that can genuinely accommodate the Principle of Worthy Intentions? Perhaps PepsiCo is just ahead of its time. "The challenge will be the transition period," said PepsiCo's Global Nutrition Group head, Dr. Mehmood Khan, in 2010. "I think once you evolve through this transition period, you'll find the efficiencies, you'll find the opportunities and you'll reset or reframe yourself. . . . Whether you're an individual or a company, if you're willing to reinvent, you've got a long, long runway ahead."[17]

For companies that aren't in the shareholder bind faced by the management of large, publicly traded companies, a new vehicle can shorten Khan's proverbial runway: the benefit corporation (B corporation). This new type of corporate entity has its roots in the corporations chartered by the states in the early days of America to create public benefits like canals, bridges, and roads. Their shareholders were allowed to take profits, but their source of legitimacy lay in their advancing of the common good.

Similarly, today's benefit corporations are certainly allowed to earn profits, but the state statutes under which they are incorporated typically require them to do three other things: (1) create a material positive impact on society, (2) consider nonfinancial interests as part of their fiduciary duty when making decisions, and (3) report on their social and environmental performance using credible, independent, and transparent third-party standards.[18] In April 2010, Maryland became the first U.S. state to pass benefit corporation legislation, and eleven states followed suit, with similar legislation introduced in six states and the District of Columbia.

Enacted within the framework of the states' existing corporate statutes, the laws governing benefit corporations offer broad legal protection to directors and officers. And they offer a flexible framework that can accommodate for-profit enterprises whose social purposes are central to their existence. The benefit corporation not only enables company management to practice worthy intentions toward customers and other stakeholders without fear of reprisals from shareholders, but also, in essence, *requires* them to behave selflessly. In a sense, that dual focus—freeing corporations to pursue worthy goals and creating a legal framework to compel them to do so—could be said to institutionalize the dynamics of the Michelangelo phenomenon. Most important for the long-term future of commerce, the benefit corporation framework enables mission-driven companies to stay mission-driven. Through leadership successions, capital raises, and changes in ownership, the benefit corporation structure can institutionalize the values, culture, and high standards put in place by the company's original founding entrepreneurs.

Patagonia ranks among the companies leading the charge for benefit corporations. On January 3, 2012, when California's benefit corporation law went into effect, Yvon Chouinard, Patagonia's seventy-four-year-old founder, led a dozen chief executives into the secretary of state's office in Sacramento to register their companies under the new legal designation.[19] "I hope five or ten years from now we'll look back on this day and say this was the start of a revolution, because the existing paradigm isn't working anymore," said Chouinard. "This is the future."

Patagonia's advantage, as is true for many B corporations, is that it is privately held. It's doubtful that Wall Street or shareholders would have applauded such bold business moves, motivated largely by worthy intentions. And under current corporate structures, large publicly traded companies are not going to find it easy to meet the demands of the Relationship Renaissance. They may also increasingly find themselves competing with smaller, more agile companies whose existence might have been of little concern to the large corporations before the benefit corporation structure gave those smaller companies increased access to capital and the freedom to pursue the common good.

In fact, many well-known and rapidly growing companies, including Ben & Jerry's, Method, Etsy, Seventh Generation, Cabot Creamery, Dansko, and Plum Organics have adopted B corporation status—not to mention the hundreds of business-to-business firms across sixty industries and twenty-seven countries worldwide.[20] In doing so, they've chosen to complement their worthy intentions with the "verified performance" required by B corporation statutes.

The B corporation is hardly a silver bullet solution. It is, however, an example of how the Relationship Renaissance is inspiring new ways of thinking about adapting and rebalancing corporate priorities for the sustainable benefit of all their stakeholders.

Moreover, when one of the most influential business strategists of our generation declares, as Michael E. Porter did in 2011, that "the capitalist system is under siege,"[21] it's time for companies and brands to take note. From the standpoint of customers and citizens, the system appears to be breaking down. Companies can no longer control the flow of information, bad customer experiences are no longer a secret, and companies are increasingly losing out to competitors who earn fanatical loyalty from customers by forging genuine relationships with them. Most companies, with some notable exceptions, continue to violate all of the prerequisites for trust that we unconsciously expect of them. The good news is that they won't be able to do so much longer.

For much of the modern era, the relentless drive for quarterly results and the impersonality of the world of mass everything has encouraged companies to pursue business in a way that turns out to be deeply flawed. When that pursuit spills over into excess, customers inevitably jump to negative conclusions about all of the people associated with a misbehaving company or brand, even though most of those people actually wince at those perceptions and deeply wish it were otherwise.

Corporate managers should be delighted to throw out the old playbook. A number of companies already have—some instinctively grasping the principles of warmth and competence, and a few embracing them by design. For all the difficulties presented by corporate legal structures and the accompanying investment culture in which large companies operate, it is important to remember that the vast majority of business people want to "be good" and "do good." Human nature favors the movement toward a business culture of worthy intentions.

Research tells us that when people are able to act in ways consistent with their ideals, they enjoy enhanced personal well-being, including greater life satisfaction and psychological health.[22] Research also shows that people prefer to work for companies with worthy intentions: according to a 2011 survey of more than 750 MBA graduates, 88 percent said they would be willing to take a pay cut to work for a company that has ethical businesses practices versus one that does not.[23]

The conclusion is unavoidable: in this age when reputations can be made and broken around the world in a single day, our capacity to express warmth and competence is among our most precious assets. It follows that the most natural and sustainable way to achieve any kind of meaningful success—personal, professional, or commercial—is to earn the lasting loyalty of others by keeping their best interests at the center of everything we do. Doing so doesn't require that we recklessly disregard our own interests. Rather, it recognizes that our success as humans has always depended on the cooperation and loyalty of others. In that regard, keeping the best interests of others in balance with our own is simply a form of enlightened self-interest. It's a mindset that embraces the warmth-and-competence perceptions that drive our choices and shape the human brand in each of us.

Notes

Introduction

1. *Survivor* wins big ratings. (2000, August 25). *San Francisco Chronicle*.
2. Wojciszke, B., et al. (1998). On the dominance of moral categories in impression formation. *Personality & Social Psychology Bulletin, 24,* 1245–1257.
3. Leach, W. (1993). *Land of desire: Merchants, power, and the rise of a new American culture.* New York: Pantheon, 7.
4. Ibid, 123.
5. Swann, W. B., Gómez, Á., Seyle, D. C., Morales, J. F., & Huici, C. (2009, May). Identity fusion: The interplay of personal and social identities in extreme group behavior. *Journal of Personality and Social Psychology, 96*(5), 995–1011.
6. Tedlow, R. (1990). *New and improved: The story of mass marketing in America.* New York: Basic Books, 271.
7. Leach, 42.
8. Fiske, S., & Taylor, S. E. (2013). *Social cognition: From brains to culture.* Los Angeles: SAGE.
9. Anywhere the eye can see, it's likely to see an ad. (2007, January 15). *New York Times.*
10. Larson, E. (1992). *The naked consumer: How our private lives become public commodities.* New York: Holt.
11. Lagniappe: A little extra. (2009, January). *A lesson on English.* Retrieved from www.ili.cc/images/ALOE_2009_January_Lagniappe.pdf
12. Baumeister, R. F., & Leary, M. R. (1995, May). *Psychological Bulletin, 117*(3), 497–529.
13. Rainie, L., & Wellman, B. (2012). *Networked: The new social operating system.* Cambridge, MA: MIT Press, 197.

14. Verizon Wireless cancels $2 "convenience fee" after backlash. (2011, December 20). Retrieved from http://www.bloomberg.com/news/2011-12-30/verizon-defends-2-convenience-fee-.html

15. Can Honest Tea say no to Coke, its biggest investor? (2010, July 7). *New York Times.*

16. Peter Kaye interview with Chris Malone, August 9, 2011.

Chapter One

1. Fiske & Taylor, *Social cognition* (see Introduction, n. 8).

2. Shaich stepping down as Panera CEO in May. (2009, November 18). *St. Louis Business Journal.*

3. Wojciszke, B. (1998). On the dominance of moral categories in impression formation. *Personality and Social Psychology Bulletin, 24,* 1245–1257.

4. Willis, J., & Todorov, A. (2006). First impressions: Making up your mind after a 100-ms exposure to a face. *Psychological Science, 17*(7), 592–598.

5. Ibid.

6. Todorov, A., Said, C. P., Engel, A. D., & Oosterhof, N. N. (2008). Understanding evaluation of faces on social dimensions. *Trends in Cognitive Sciences, 12*(12), 455–460. On babyfaces, see Zebrowitz, L. A., & Montepare, J. M. (1992). Impressions of babyfaced individuals across the life span. *Developmental Psychology, 28*(6), 1143–1152.

7. Todorov, A., Mandisodza, A. N., Goren, A., & Hall, C. C. (2005). Inferences of competence from faces predict election outcomes. *Science, 308*(5728), 1623–1626.

8. Banaji, M. R., & Gelman, S. A. (2013). *Navigating the social world: What infants, children, and other species can teach us.* New York: Oxford University Press.

9. Harlow, H. F. (1958). The nature of love. *American Psychologist, 13*(12), 673–685. Harlow, H. F., & Zimmermann, R. R. (1959). Affectional responses in the infant monkey. *Science, 130,* 421–432.

10. Bargh, J. A., & Shalev, I. (2012). The substitutability of physical and social warmth in daily life. *Emotion, 12*(1), 154–162. Zhong, C.-B., & Leonardelli, G. J. (2008). Cold and lonely: Does social exclusion literally feel cold? *Psychological Science, 19*(9), 838–842. IJzerman, H., & Semin, G. R. (2010). Temperature perceptions as a ground for social proximity. *Journal of Experimental Social Psychology, 46*(6), 867–873. Vess, M. (2012). Warm thoughts: Attachment anxiety and sensitivity to temperature cues. *Psychological Science, 23*(5), 472–47. Kang, Y., Williams, L. E., Clark,

M. S., Gray, J. R., & Bargh, J. A. (2011). Physical temperature effects on trust behavior: The role of insula. *Social Cognitive and Affective Neuroscience, 6*(4), 507–515.

11. Williams, L. E., & Bargh, J. A. (2008). Experiencing physical warmth promotes interpersonal warmth. *Science, 322*(5901), 606–607.

12. Stulp, G., Buunk, A. P., Verhulst, S., & Pollet, T. V. (2012). Tall claims? Sense and nonsense about the importance of height of US presidents. *The Leadership Quarterly.*

13. Schubert, T. W. (2005). Your highness: Vertical positions as perceptual symbols of power. *Journal of Personality and Social Psychology, 89,* 1–21.

14. Tiedens, L. Z., & Fragale, A. R. (2003). Power moves: Complementarity in dominant and submissive nonverbal behavior. *Journal of Personality and Social Psychology, 84*(3), 558–568.

15. Schubert, T. W., & Koole, S. L. (2009). The embodied self: Making a fist enhances men's power-related self-conceptions. *Journal of Experimental Social Psychology, 45*(4), 828–834. Schubert, T. W. (2004). The power in your hand: Gender differences in bodily feedback from making a fist. *Personality and Social Psychology Bulletin, 30*(6), 757–769.

16. Carney, D. R., Cuddy, A. J. C., & Yap, A. J. (2010). Power posing: Brief nonverbal displays affect neuroendocrine levels and risk tolerance. *Psychological Science, 21*(10), 1363–1368.

17. Kervyn, N., Fiske, S. T., & Yzerbyt, Y. (Under review). *Why is the primary dimension of social cognition so hard to predict? Symbolic and realistic threats together predict warmth in the stereotype content model.* Note that warmth includes two highly correlated dimensions, one being sociability and the other morality. While exceptions exist (a con man is highly sociable but immoral), in practice, they tend to go together.

18. Abele, A. E. (2003). The dynamics of masculine-agentic and feminine-communal traits: findings from a prospective study. *Journal of Personality and Social Psychology, 85,* 768–776. Asch, S. E. (1946). Forming impressions of personality. *Journal of Abnormal and Social Psychology, 42,* 258–290. Bales, R. F. (1950). A set of categories for the analysis of small group interaction. *American Sociological Review, 15,* 257–263. Rosenberg, S. (1968). A multidimensional approach to the structure of personality impressions. *Journal of Personality and Social Psychology, 9,* 283–294.

19. Fiske, S. T., Cuddy, A. J. C., Glick, P., & Xu, J. (2002). A model of (often mixed) stereotype content: Competence and warmth respectively follow from perceived status and competition. *Journal of Personality and Social Psychology, 82,* 878–902. Cuddy, A. J. C., Fiske, S. T., & Glick, P. (2007).

The BIAS map: Behaviors from intergroup affect and stereotypes. *Journal of Personality and Social Psychology, 92,* 631–648.

20. Cuddy, A. J. C., Fiske, S. T., Kwan, V. S. Y., Glick, P., Demoulin, S., Leyens, J-Ph., . . . Ziegler, R. (2009). Stereotype content model across cultures: Towards universal similarities and some differences. *British Journal of Social Psychology, 48,* 1–33. Durante, F., Fiske, S. T., Kervyn, N., Cuddy, A. J. C., Akande, A., Adetoun, B. E., . . . Storari, C. C. (2013). Nations' income inequality predicts ambivalence in stereotype content: How societies mind the gap. *British Journal of Social Psychology.* Fiske et al., 2002.

21. Fiske, S. T. (1998). Stereotyping, prejudice, and discrimination. In D. T. Gilbert, S. T. Fiske, & G. Lindzey (Eds.), *Handbook of social psychology* (4th ed., Vol. 2, pp. 357–411). New York: McGraw-Hill. Fiske & Taylor, 2013, Chapter 11. Macrae, C. N., & Bodenhausen, G. V. (2000). Social cognition: Thinking categorically about others. *Annual Review of Psychology, 51,* 93–120.

22. Fiske, S. T. (2011). *Envy up, scorn down: How status divides us.* New York: Russell Sage Foundation.

23. Fournier, S. (1998). Consumers and their brands: Developing relationship theory in consumer research. *Journal of Consumer Research, 24,* 343–373. Fournier, S. (2009). Lessons learned about consumers' relationships with their brands. In J. Priester, D. MacInnis, & C. W. Park (Eds.), *Handbook of brand relationships* (pp. 5–23). New York: Society for Consumer Psychology & M. E. Sharp. Aaker, J. (1997). Dimensions of brand personality. *Journal of Marketing Research, 34*(3), 347–356.

24. Ahuvia, A. C. (2005). Beyond the extended self: Loved objects and consumers' identity narratives. *Journal of Consumer Research, 32*(1), 171–184. Albert, N., Merunka, D., & Valette-Florence, P. (2010). *Passion for the brand and consumer brand relationships.* Dunedin, NZ: Australian and New Zealand Marketing Academy. Thomson, M., MacInnis, D. J., & Park, C. W. (2005). The ties that bind: Measuring the strength of consumers' emotional attachments to brands. *Journal of Consumer Psychology, 15,* 77–91.

25. Kervyn, N., Fiske, S. T., & Malone, C. (2012). Brands as intentional agents framework: Warmth and competence map brand perception. Target Article, *Journal of Consumer Psychology, 22,* 166–176.

26. Nass, C., Moon, Y., Fogg, B., Reeves, B., & Dryer, C. (1995). Can computer personalities be human personalities? *International Journal of*

Human–Computer Studies, 43, 223–239. Nass, C., Moon, Y., & Carney, P. (1999). Are people polite to computers? Responses to computer-based interviewing systems. *Journal of Applied Social Psychology, 29*(5), 1093–1110. Nass, C., & Moon, Y. (2000). Machines and mindlessness: Social responses to computers. *Journal of Social Issues, 56*(1), 81–103.

27. Karr-Wisniewski, P., & Prietula, M. (2010). CASA, WASA, and the dimensions of us. *Computers in Human Behavior, 26*, 1761–1771.

Chapter Two

1. Peeters, G. (1991). Relational information processing and the implicit personality concept. *Cahiers de Psychologie Cognitive/Current Psychology of Cognition, 11*(2), 259–278. Wojciszke, B. (1994). Multiple meanings of behavior: construing actions in terms of competence or morality. *Journal of Personality and Social Psychology* 67, 222–232.

2. Clark, M. S., & Mills, J. (1979). Interpersonal attraction in exchange and communal relationships. *Journal of Personality and Social Psychology, 37*(1), 12–24. Fiske, A. P. (1991). *Structures of social life: The four elementary forms of human relations: Communal sharing, authority ranking, equality matching, market pricing.* New York: Free Press. Fiske, A. P. (1992). The four elementary forms of sociality: Framework for a unified theory of social relations. *Psychological Review, 99*(4), 689–723.

3. Gerbasi, M. E., & Prentice, D. A. (in press). The self- and other-interest inventory. *Journal of Personality and Social Psychology.*

4. Sprint plans for end of Nextel push-to-talk network. (2012, June 18). *Kansas City Star.* Retrieved from http://www.kansascity.com/2012/06/18/3664694/sprint-plans-for-end-of-nextel.html#storylink=cpy

5. CNET.com. (2007, July 5). Retrieved from http://news.cnet.com/8301-10784_3-9739869-7.html

6. Bedeviled by the churn, Sprint tries to win back disgruntled customers. (2008, July 8). *New York Times.*

7. Sprint Nextel makes strides to improve image. (2010, June 29). CNET.com. Retrieved from http://news.cnet.com/8301-30686_3-20009100-266.html

8. Sprint news release. (2012, May 15). Retrieved from http://newsroom.sprint.com/article_display.cfm?article_id=2282

9. Ibid.

10. *Fair Disclosure Wire.* (2012, May 16). Sprint Nextel teleconference call, J.P. Morgan TMT Conference 2012.

11. Reichheld, F., & Teal, T. (1996). *The loyalty effect: The hidden force behind growth, profits, and lasting value*. Boston, MA: Harvard Business School Press.
12. Frequent-flyer miles in terminal decline? (2006, January 6). *Economist*.
13. Hayashi, F. (2009). Do U.S. consumers really benefit from payment card rewards? *Economic Review*. Retrieved from http://www.kansascityfed.org/PUBLICAT/ECONREV/PDF/09q1Hayashi.pdf
14. Love those loyalty programs: But who reaps the real rewards? (2007, April 4). *Knowledge@Wharton*. Retrieved from http://knowledge.wharton.upenn.edu/article.cfm?articleid=1700
15. Cialdini, R. B. (1993). *Influence: Science and practice* (3rd ed.). New York: HarperCollins College.
16. Whatever happened to Green Stamps? (2001, July 24). *The Straight Dope*. Retrieved from http://www.straightdope.com/columns/read/1940/whatever-happened-to-green-stamps
17. Strativity Group 2010 Customer Experience Management Survey.
18. Love those loyalty programs, 2007.
19. Bob Dekoy interview by Chris Malone, January 9, 2013.

Chapter Three

1. This woman spent $15,000 on Lululemon and she doesn't even do yoga. (2012, September 18). *Business Insider*. Retrieved from http://www.businessinsider.com/lululemon-addict-why-she-buys-2012-9#ixzz2QS1N9Roe
2. The long and the short of it: Complimentary hemming. Retrieved from http://www.lululemon.com/community/blog/complimentary-hemming/
3. RetalSails report. Retrieved from http://www.retailsails.com/index.php/site/reports
4. Wallace, E. (2009). *Business relationships that last*. Austin, TX: Greenleaf Book Group Press, 13.
5. Yamagishi, T. (1998). *Trust: The evolutionary game of mind and society*. Tokyo: Tokyo University Press.
6. Gurtman, M. B. (1992). Trust, distrust, and interpersonal problems: A circumplex analysis. *Journal of Personality and Social Psychology*, 62, 989–1002. Murray, S. L., & Holmes, J. G. (1993). Seeing virtues as faults: Negativity and the transformation of interpersonal narratives in close relationships. *Journal of Personality and Social Psychology*, 65, 707–722. Morling, B., & Fiske, S. T. (1999). Defining and measuring harmony

control. *Journal of Research in Personality, 33*, 379–414. Rotenberg, K. J. (1994). Loneliness and interpersonal trust. *Journal of Social and Clinical Psychology, 13*, 152–173. Rotter, J. B. (1980). Interpersonal trust, trustworthiness, and gullibility. *American Psychologist, 35*, 17.

7. Orbell, J. M., & Dawes, R. M. (1993). Social welfare, cooperators' advantage, and the option of not playing the game. *American Sociological Review, 58*, 787–800.

8. For a review, see Fiske, S. T. (2010). *Social beings: A core motives approach to social psychology* (2nd ed.). New York: Wiley. All else being equal, people expect basically good outcomes, especially from other people. People are biased to see the best in other people; although people differ, mostly they trust other people to be basically benign. See also Matlin, M. W., & Stang, D. J. (1978). *The Pollyanna Principle.* Cambridge, MA: Schenkman. Parducci, A. (1968). The relativism of absolute judgments. *Scientific American, 219*, 84–90. Sears, D. O. (1983). The person-positivity bias. *Journal of Personality and Social Psychology, 44*, 233–250.

9. Boon, S. D. (1995). Trust. In A. S. R. Manstead & M. Hewstone (Eds.), *Blackwell encyclopedia of social psychology* (pp. 656–657). Oxford: Blackwell.

10. Lululemon's secret sauce. (2012, March 12). *Wall Street Journal.*

11. Ibid.

12. Krueger, F., McCabe, K., Moll, J., Kriegeskorte, N., Zahn, R., Strenziok, M., & Grafman, J. (2007). Neural correlates of trust. *PNAS: Proceedings of the National Academy of Sciences of the United States of America, 104*, 20084–20089.

13. Ibid.

14. Luluemon yoga pants make comeback after recall. (2013, June 3). *Wall Street Journal.* Retrieved from http://online.wsj.com/article/SB1000142412 78873234698045785237901033376784.html

15. CEO bows out at Lululemon. (2013, June 10). *Wall Street Journal.* Retrieved from http://online.wsj.com/article/SB100014241278873246343 04578537712064607592.html?mod=WSJ_qtoverview_wsjlatest#article Tabs%3Darticle

16. Baumeister, R. F., & Leary, M. R. (1995). The need to belong: Desire for interpersonal attachments as a fundamental human motivation. *Psychological Bulletin, 117*, 497–529. See Fiske (2010; n. 8) for other sources.

17. Zane, C. (2011). *Reinventing the wheel: The science of creating lifetime customers.* Dallas, TX: BenBella Books, 51.

18. Ibid., 37.
19. Fiske, S. T. (2011). *Envy up, scorn down: How status divides us.* New York: Russell Sage Foundation.
20. Feather, N. T. (1999). Judgments of deservingness: Studies in the psychology of justice and achievement. *Personality and Social Psychology Review, 3*(2), 86–107.
21. Interview with Harry Smith, *Rock Center,* NBC-TV, December 13, 2012.
22. Ibid.
23. Chobani debuts first-ever national advertising campaign. (2011, February 17). PR Newswire.
24. Who we are. (n.d.). Chobani. Retrieved from http://chobani.com/who-we-are/
25. Transcript of Hamdi Ulukaya interview on *Bloomberg Surveillance.* (2011, November 10). Bloomberg TV network.

Chapter Four

1. Groupon in retrospect. (2010, September 17). Posies Bakery and Café blog. Retrieved from http://posiescafe.com/wp/groupon-in-retrospect/
2. Groupon satisfaction rate not so hot, study finds. (2010, September 30). WSJ.com. Retrieved from http://blogs.wsj.com/digits/2010/09/30/rice-university-study-groupon-renewal-rate-not-so-hot/
3. The REAL data on Groupon's performance. (2011, June 7). DylanCollins.com. Retrieved from http://dylancollins.com/?p=297
4. Groupon in retrospect.
5. Bargh, J. A., & McKenna, K. Y. A. (2004). The Internet and social life. *Annual Review of Psychology, 55,* 573–590. http://www.annualreviews.org/doi/abs/10.1146/annurev.psych.55.090902.141922
6. Down with loyalty cards: Another view. (2012, September 21). Couponsinthenews.com. Retrieved from http://couponsinthenews.com/2012/09/21/down-with-loyalty-cards-another-view/
7. Karr-Wisniewski, P., & Prietula, M. (2010). CASA, WASA and the dimensions of US. *Computers in Human Behavior, 26,* 1761–1771.
8. Ibid.
9. Zappos' outrageous record for the longest customer service phone call ever. (2012, December 20). *Business Insider.* Retrieved from http://www.businessinsider.com/zappos-longest-customer-service-call-2012-12#ixzz2QTtZ2EmG
10. Zappos CEO letter. Retrieved from http://blogs.zappos.com/amazonclosing

11. The notice is at Endless.com
12. Accenture 2011 Global Consumer Research Study. Retrieved from http://www.accenture.com/SiteCollectionDocuments/PDF/Accenture-Global-Consumer-Research-New-Realities.pdf
13. Charlie Rose interview with John Donahoe. (2013, February 5). Retrieved from http://www.charlierose.com/view/interview/12764
14. How top brands tackle customer service on Twitter. (2012, December 5). *Simply Measured*. Retrieved from http://simplymeasured.com/blog/2012/12/05/23-of-top-brands-have-a-dedicated-customer-service-handle-on-twitter-study/
15. Ibid.

Chapter Five

1. Domino's Pizza Turnaround. Retrieved from http://www.youtube.com/watch?v=AH5R56jILag
2. Russell Weiner interview with Chris Malone, October 5, 2012.
3. Pizza turnaround case study, Advertising Research Foundation. Retrieved from http://www.thearf.org/ogilvy-11-winners
4. Russell Weiner interview.
5. The many acts of Domino's Pizza. (2010, August). *QSR Magazine*. Retrieved from http://www.qsrmagazine.com/menu-innovations/many-acts-domino-s-pizza
6. Russell Weiner interview.
7. Ibid.
8. Get ready for prime time. (2012, August). *QSR Magazine*. Retrieved from http://www.qsrmagazine.com/executive-insights/get-ready-prime-time
9. Adams, S. (2011, November 30). Steve Jobs tops list of 2011's most buzzed about CEO. Forbes Leadership Blog. Retrieved from http://www.forbes.com/sites/susanadams/2011/11/30/ceos-with-the-best-and-worst-online-buzz/
10. Brady, D. (2012, July 26). God and gay marriage. *Businessweek*.
11. Hsu, T. (2013, January 17). Whole Foods CEO regrets comparing Obamacare to fascism. *Los Angeles Times*.
12. Harry Woods, partner-creative director at Woods Witt Dealy & Sons, quoted in Parekh, R. (2009, September 14). Ten things to think hard about before featuring the chairman in advertising. *Advertising Age*.
13. Fiske, S. T., & Dépret, E. (1996). Control, interdependence, and power: Understanding social cognition in its social context. In

W. Stroebe & M. Hewstone (Eds.), *European review of social psychology* (Vol. 7, pp. 31–61). New York: Wiley. Dépret, E. F., & Fiske, S. T. (1999). Perceiving the powerful: Intriguing individuals versus threatening groups. *Journal of Experimental Social Psychology, 35*, 461–480. Stevens, L. E., & Fiske, S. T. (2000). Motivated impressions of a powerholder: Accuracy under task dependency and misperception under evaluative dependency. *Personality and Social Psychology Bulletin, 26*, 907–922.

14. Fazio, R. H., & Zanna, M. P. (1978). Attitudinal qualities relating to the strength of the attitude-behavior relationship. *Journal of Experimental Social Psychology, 14*, 398–408. Fazio, R. H., & Zanna, M. P. (1981). Direct experience and attitude-behavior consistency. In L. Berkowitz (Ed.), *Advances in experimental social psychology* (Vol. 14, pp. 162–203). New York: Academic Press.

15. CEOs in advertisements. (2012, March 3). AceMetrix.com. Retrieved from www.acemetrix.com/spotlights/insights

16. Celebrity advertisements: Exposing a myth of advertising effectiveness. (2011, January 1). AceMetrix.com. Retrieved from www.acemetrix.com/spotlights/insights

17. Ibid., 7–8.

18. The Prosumer Report: The future of the corporate brand (Vol. 4). (2008). Retrieved from http://www.slideshare.net/eurorscgww/the-future-of-the-corporate-brand

19. Bass, B. M. (1990). From transactional to transformational leadership: Learning to share the vision. *Organizational Dynamics, 18*, 19–31.

20. Ibid., 24.

21. Russell Weiner interview.

22. Ibid.

23. Tate Dillow: The man behind Domino's new chicken. (2011, February 28). Retrieved from http://www.youtube.com/watch?v=ghc8b8LRmMQ

24. Russell Weiner interview.

25. Ibid.

26. Ibid.

27. Retrieved from http://www.facebook.com/Dominos/app_251180338316991

28. Retrieved from http://more.dominos.com/show-us-your-pizza-sunset/www/images/gallery/desktop/img.show_us_your_pizza_photo_6_by_geoff_r.jpg

29. Retrieved from http://more.dominos.com/show-us-your-pizza-sunset/www/images/gallery/desktop/img.show_us_your_pizza_photo_6_by_ania_g.jpg

30. Domino's show us your pizza. (2011, February 17). Retrieved from http://www.youtube.com/watch?v=Aqy8mAs-Izk

31. Russell Weiner interview.

32. Kelman, H. C. (1958). Compliance, identification, and internalization: Three processes of attitude change. *The Journal of Conflict Resolution, 2*(1), 51–60.

33. Fiske & Taylor, 2013.

34. Tim Cost interview with Chris Malone, February 2, 2013.

35. Ibid.

36. Hogg, M. A. (2001). A social identity theory of leadership. *Personality and Social Psychology Review, 5*(3), 184–200.

37. Hains, S. C., Hogg, M. A., & Duck, J. M. (1997). Self-categorization and leadership: Effects of group prototypicality and leader stereotypicality. *Personality and Social Psychology Bulletin, 23,* 1087–1100.

38. Malone, C. (2011, June). Phase 3 Brand Warmth & Competence Study.

39. Mar, R. A. (2011). The neural bases of social cognition and story comprehension. *Annual Review of Psychology, 62,* 103–134.

40. Quirk, M. B. (2011, March 30). Debunking the creation myths behind 5 huge companies. *Consumerist.* Retrieved from http://consumerist.com/2011/03/30/the-creation-myths-startups-told-to-get-a-foot-in-the-door/

41. Cassano, E. (2011, September 1). How Patrick Doyle faced the reality of not being the best—and took steps to put Domino's back on top. *Smart Business Network.* Retrieved from http://www.sbnonline.com/2011/09/how-patrick-doyle-faced-the-reality-of-not-being-the-best---and-took-steps-to-put-domino's-back-on-top/

42. Vandello, J. A., Goldschmied, N. P., & Richards, D. A. R. (2007, December). The appeal of the underdog. *Personality and Social Psychology Bulletin, 33*(12), 1603–1616.

43. Ben and Jerry's to Unilever, with attitude. (2000, April 13). *New York Times.*

44. Retrieved from http://www.benjerry.com/company/timeline

45. Ibid.

46. Ben and Jerry's to Unilever, 2000.

47. How Richard Branson works magic. (1998, October 1). *Strategy + Business,* Fourth Quarter, 13.

48. Ibid.

49. It is a very sad day—Branson. (2007, February 24). *BBC News.* Retrieved from http://news.bbc.co.uk/2/hi/uk_news/6392935.stm

50. Ibid.

51. Ibid.

Chapter Six

1. Prior driver of Lexus says pedal stuck; Sheriff report faults mats in Aug. crash. (2009, December 5). *San Diego Union-Tribune*.
2. Ibid.
3. CHP releases 911 call in officer's fiery crash. (2009, September 10). *San Diego Union-Tribune*.
4. Fatal Toyota crash detailed. (2009, October 25). *Los Angeles Times*.
5. Polk & Co. (2010, January 13). Retrieved from http://polk.phirebranding.com/company/news/polk_announces_2009_model_year_automotive_loyalty_award_winnersR
6. 2009 Auto Reliability Study. (2009, October 29). Retrieved from ConsumerReports.org
7. Fatal Toyota crash detailed. (2009, October 25). *Los Angeles Times*.
8. "Like a car on a slingshot." (2010, February 28). *Los Angeles Times*.
9. Fatal Toyota crash detailed. (2009, October 25). *Los Angeles Times*.
10. Toyota gets intense new scrutiny. (2010, February 17). *Los Angeles Times*.
11. Toyota cited $100 million savings after limiting recall. (2010, February 22). *New York Times*.
12. Toyota's focus was recall costs. (2010, February 22). *Los Angeles Times*.
13. An apology from Toyota's leader. (2010, February 25). *New York Times*.
14. Toyota on pace to outsell all its rivals worldwide. (2012, November 24). *Los Angeles Times*.
15. Toyota gets intense new U.S. scrutiny. (2010, February 17). *Los Angeles Times*.
16. Toyota on pace to outsell all its rivals worldwide. (2012, November 24). *Los Angeles Times*.
17. Toyota tries to get back on track. (2010, February 2). *Los Angeles Times*.
18. House of Representatives Committee on Oversight and Government Reform. (2010, February 24).
19. Tylenol's rapid comeback. (1983, September 17). *New York Times*.
20. Children's Tylenol and other drugs recalled.(2010, May 1). *New York Times*.
21. What's ailing J&J—and why isn't its rep hurting? (2010, May 10). *Advertising Age*.
22. This chart is a composite of seven separate studies conducted by the authors between July, 2010 and February, 2013 with over 5,000 U.S. adults. However, some of these studies had differing sample sizes and methodologies, so the data have been normalized to account for these differences. Nonetheless, this chart is intended for illustration purposes only and should not be considered definitive. It should also be noted that while interesting,

this chart is a relative comparison of how the U.S. adult population views these companies and brands, and therefore is not necessarily representative of the customers that actually purchase these products and services. Importantly though, it reflects a pattern of perceptions and emotions that is very similar to that found in social perception studies of human stereotypes and bias. This strongly suggests that warmth and competence are guiding our thoughts and behavior in both contexts.

23. Consumers steer clear of the Audi 5000 S. (1986, December 28). *Washington Post.*

24. Ibid.

25. Toyota recall costs: $2 billion. (2010, May 1). *New York Times.*

26. Toyota to pay $1.1 billion in recall case. (2012, December 26). *CNN Wire.*

27. *Proverbs* 16:18.

28. Exline, J. J., Baumeister, R. F., Bushman, B. J., Campbell, W. K., & Finkel, E. J. (2004). Too proud to let go: Narcissistic entitlement as a barrier to forgiveness. *Journal of Personality and Social Psychology, 87*(6), 894–912.

29. Levinson, W. (1997, February 19). Physician-patient communication: The relationship with malpractice claims among primary care physicians and surgeons. *Journal of the American Medical Association, 277*(7), 553–59.

30. Brennan, T. (1996, December 26). Relation between negligent adverse events and the outcomes of medical-malpractice litigation. *New England Journal of Medicine, 335*(26), 1963–67.

31. Helmreich, R., Aronson, E., & LeFan, J. (1970). To err is humanizing sometimes: Effects of self-esteem, competence, and a pratfall on interpersonal attraction. *Journal of Personality and Social Psychology, 16*(2), 259–264.

32. There were exceptions, though, in the reactions of student test subjects who, in a personality test, ranked either exceptionally high or exceptionally low in self-esteem. Among these particular students, those who saw the highly competent applicant spill the coffee actually ranked him *lower* for likeability. Researchers could only speculate that among extremely high-self-esteem subjects, the coffee spill was taken as a sign of inferior status, while the low-self-esteem subjects possibly have rigidly high expectations for people of high accomplishments.

33. Cook, T. (n.d.). To our customers. Retrieved from http://www.apple.com/letter-from-tim-cook-on-maps/

34. Epstein, Z. (2012, September 20). Apple's iOS 6 Maps App is awful, and now the world knows it. BGR.com. Retrieved from http://bgr.com/2012/09/20/apples-ios-6-maps-criticism/

35. Tim Cook interview with Brian Williams (2012, December 6). *Rock Center*, NBC-TV.

36. J&J recall watch: More musty-smelling Tylenol caplets. (2011, March 29). *Wall Street Journal*.

37. The full text of the Johnson & Johnson credo can be retrieved from http://www.jnj.com/connect/about-jnj/jnj-credo/

38. McCullough, M. E., Rachal, K. C., Sandage, S. J., Worthington, E. L., Jr., Brown, S. Wade, & Hight, T. L. (1998, December). Interpersonal forgiving in close relationships II: Theoretical elaboration and measurement. *Journal of Personality and Social Psychology*, 75(6) 1586–1603. http://www.psy.miami.edu/faculty/mmccullough/Papers/ Interpers%20Forgiving_II.pdf

39. Ibid.

40. Liker, J., & Ogden, T. N. (2011). *Toyota under fire: Lessons for turning crisis into opportunity* (loc. 3186). New York: McGraw-Hill.

41. Johnson & Johnson recalls Infants' Tylenol. (2012, February 17). *New York Times*.

Chapter Seven

1. Duhigg, C. (2012, February 19). Psst, you in Aisle 5. *New York Times Magazine*.

2. You're getting scroogled. (2013, February 13). *Wall Street Journal*.

3. Rusbult, C. E., Finkel, E. J., & Kumashiro, M. (2009). The Michelangelo phenomenon. *Current Directions in Psychological Science*, 18(6), 305–309.

4. Schlosser, E. (2001). *Fast food nation: The dark side of the All-American meal*. Boston: Houghton Mifflin.

5. Full text of the "What's Wrong with McDonald's" pamphlet retrieved from http://www.mcspotlight.org/case/pretrial/factsheet.html

6. Drucker, P. (1993). *Post-capitalist society*. New York: HarperCollins, 72.

7. Porter, M. E., & Kramer, M. R. (2006, December). Strategy and society: The link between competitive advantage and corporate social responsibility. *Harvard Business Review*.

8. Performance with purpose. (2006). PepsiCo annual report.

9. Kanter, R. M., Khurana, R., Lal, R., & Baldwin, E. (2012, January 30). *Harvard Business School Case: PepsiCo, performance with purpose, achieving the right global balance*. Harvard Business School, 6.

10. Performance with purpose.

11. Kanter, Khurana, Lal, & Baldwin, 2012.
12. Ibid.
13. Wartzman, R. (2012, April 9). The Pepsi challenge. *Forbes* online. Retrieved from http://www.forbes.com/sites/drucker/2012/04/09/the-pepsi-challenge/
14. 204 Mich. 459, 507, 170 N.W. 668, 684 (1919). Quoted in Clark, W. H., Jr., Vranka, L., et al. (2013, January 13). The need and rationale for the benefit corporation: Why it is the legal form that best addresses the needs of social entrepreneurs, investors, and, ultimately, the public. White paper, 7.
15. Ibid., pp. 9–10.
16. Porter, M. E., & Kramer, M. R. (2011, January). Creating shared value. *Harvard Business Review.*
17. Kanter, Khurana, Lal, & Baldwin, 13.
18. Clark, Vranka, et al.
19. Lifsher, M. (2012, January 4). Businesses seek state's new "benefit corporation" status. *Los Angeles Times.*
20. B corporation statistics as of May 28, 2013. Retrieved from http://www.bcorporation.net/community
21. Porter & Kramer.
22. Drigotas, S. M. (2002). The Michelangelo phenomenon and personal well-being. *Journal of Personality, 70,* 59–77.
23. New MBAs would sacrifice pay for ethics. (2011, May 17). *Harvard Business Review,* The Daily Stat.

About the Authors

Chris Malone is founder and managing partner of Fidelum Partners, a research-based consulting and professional services firm that helps clients achieve sustained business growth and performance.

As a consultant and keynote speaker, he has worked with hundreds of senior executives in organizations ranging from Fortune 500 companies to start-ups and non-profits. Chris has over twenty years of sales, marketing, consulting, and organizational leadership experience, and a track record of driving growth and profitability. He was chief marketing officer at Choice Hotels International and senior vice president of marketing at ARAMARK Corporation, and has held senior marketing and sales positions at leading organizations including the Coca-Cola Company, the National Basketball Association, and Procter & Gamble.

Chris holds a bachelor's degree from the University of Maryland at College Park and an MBA from the Wharton School of the University of Pennsylvania. He lives in the Philadelphia area with his wife and three sons.

For more information, please visit www.TheHumanBrand .com or www.Fidelum.com. Chris can also be reached at Chris@ fidelum.com or on Twitter@hcmalone.

• • •

Susan T. Fiske is Eugene Higgins Professor, Psychology and Public Affairs at Princeton University. She investigates social cognition—especially groups' images and the emotions they create—at cultural, interpersonal, and neuroscientific levels. She is author of over three hundred publications and winner of numerous scientific awards, including election to the National Academy of Science. Most recently she has edited *Beyond Common Sense: Psychological Science in the Courtroom* (2008), the *Handbook of Social Psychology* (2010, 5/e), the *Sage Handbook of Social Cognition* (2012), and *Facing Social Class: How Societal Rank Influences Interaction* (2012). Currently she is an editor of *Annual Review of Psychology*, *Science*, and *Psychological Review*.

Susan has written two upper-level texts: *Social Cognition* (2013, 4/e) and *Social Beings: Core Motives in Social Psychology* (2014, 3/e). Sponsored by a Guggenheim, her 2011 Russell-Sage-Foundation book is *Envy Up, Scorn Down: How Status Divides Us*. Her graduate students arranged for her winning Princeton University's Mentoring Award.

Susan holds a Ph.D. from Harvard University and honorary doctorates from the Université Catholique de Louvain-la-Neuve, Belgium, and Universiteit Leiden, Netherlands. She lives with her demographer husband, Doug Massey, in Princeton and Vermont, with visits from their three children and their families.

For more information, please visit www.fiskelab.org.

Index

A

Aaker, Jennifer, 28, 29

Accenture, 99

AceMetrix, 110–111

Advertising: brand concept in early, 9–10; CEO as spokespeople, 107–108, 110–111; Domino's, 114–116; growth in brand, 8; moving into Internet and social networks, 102–103; "Pizza Turnaround" campaign, 105–110, 114–116, 145; rapid growth without, 66. *See also* Brands

Advertising Age, 133

Advil, 29

AIG, 30, 31

Alum, Alex, 44–45

Amazon: buyout of Zappos by, 98, 122; evaluating warmth and competence of, 92–94; low prices generating loyalty at, 96–98

American Airlines, 5

Amtrak, 31

Apologies: Apple's iPhone Maps, 140–142; in business crises, 125–126, 130; Domino's public, 105–106, 111, 115, 116, 145; making public, 109, 137–140

Apple's iPhone Maps, 140–142

ARAMARK, 75

Audi, 136

Avis, 121

B

Baker's dozen, 13

Bank of America, 107, 137

Bar at the Folies-Bergère, A, 6

Bass & Co., 6

Bass, Bernard M., 113

Beauchesne, Carolyn, 61–62, 65–66, 69

Ben & Jerry's Ice Cream, 122, 167

Benefit corporations, 165–166

Best Buy, 92–94

BIAS (behaviors from intergroup affect and stereotypes), 26

Blockbuster, 5

BP (British Petroleum): confidence and loyalty to, 29; Deepwater Horizon crisis, 28–30, 31, 133; defensiveness of, 137

Brand Warmth-and-Competence Matrix, 31

Brands: applying warmth and competence theory to, 4–5,

27–34; developing concept of, 8–9; eliciting warmth and confidence, 2–3; honesty and transparency in, 16–18; human face as first, 24, 37; personal talk about, 30; philanthropic acts by, 32–34, 119–120; plotting intention and ability of, 30–31; transferring customer loyalties to, 7–10. *See also* Customer loyalty

Branson, Richard, 118, 123–126

Burger King, 28

Burke, Jessie, 86–87

Business ethics: accountability to customers, 14–15, 43–44; Domino's honesty with customers, 105–110; enforcing in medieval times, 13–14; Honest Tea's goals, 16–17; keeping customer interests in mind, 21; rebirth of preindustrial values, 15–16; sharing moral values, 75–77. *See also* Crises; Relationship Renaissance; Worthy intentions

Business Insider, 62, 95

Businesses. *See* Companies

C

Cabot Creamery, 167

Cannon, Steve, 57–58

Cathy, Dan, 107, 108

Celebrity endorsements, 110–111, 118

Change: embracing significant, 156–159; forgiveness changing motivation, 145–146; shifting priorities for, 159–168

Chick-fil-A, 107, 108

Chobani, 11

Chobani yogurt, 81–83, 159

Chouinard, Yvon, 166

Citibank, 133

Clemons, Erik, 53–54

CNET, 141

Coca-Cola: acquiring Honest Tea, 16–17; analyzing customer loyalty for, 34–36, 37, 38; branding of, 3, 11; Pepsi-Cola rankings vs., 162. *See also* Honest Tea

Comcast, 146, 148

Communal relationships, 41–42

Community: Chobani yogurt's, 82–83; developing alumni, 73–74; Lululemon's development of, 61–63, 74–75

Companies: acts of generosity from, 19–21; adding warmth to communications, 156–158; apologizing for product failures, 111, 125–126, 130, 140–142; asking for forgiveness, 109, 137, 140; becoming more self-aware, 152–156; building customer loyalty, 41–42, 47–54; changing attitude toward, 116–119; composite warmth and competence ratings for, 134; customer-based practices for, 54–57; data mining by, 154, 155; dealing with unacceptable service, 105–106, 115, 116; embracing significant change, 156–159; estimating lifetime value of customers, 79; evaluating with warmth and confidence theory, 4–5; exhibiting qualities of warmth, 39–42; gaging Internet presence for, 90–92; Groupon promotions for,

85–87; incorporating as benefit corporations, 165–166; judging on their people, 33; keeping customer interests in mind, 21; learning from mistakes, 148–150; limitations in reward programs, 50; losing customer loyalties, 10; loyalty linked with profits, 46–47; protecting reputations, 13–14; reorienting accountability to customers, 14–15, 43–44; reservoir of good will in crises, 142–145; sharing moral values within, 75–77; shifting priorities in, 159–168; slashing costs and services in, 45–46; stories about, 119–122; taking loyalty test, 153; using social networks, 56, 99–101; using worthy intentions competitively, 77–80; working for those with worthy intentions, 168; worthy intentions of, 64–67. *See also* Community; Reward programs

Competence: assessing, 22; combining with warmth at Zane's Cycles, 80; evaluating in charitable giving campaigns, 71–72; forgiving excessive, 138–140; Groupon crowding and perceived, 87; overreliance on, 8; perceiving and judging person's, 2; snap judgments on, 23–24; without warmth, 45–46; Zappos', 94–96. *See also* Warmth and competence theory

Complaints: Audi's response to, 136; demonstrating loyalty in response to, 53–54

Compliance with values, 116, 117

Cook, Brandon, 19–20

Cook, Theresa, 19–20

Cook, Tim, 140–141

Corporate culture. *See* Business ethics; Worthy intentions

Cost, Tim, 118

Costs: "Pizza Turnaround" campaign, 106; required to maintain loyalty, 46–47; reward program, 48–49; slashing company's services and, 45–46; Toyota recall, 136–137. *See also* Profitability

Crises: apologizing to customers in, 125–126, 130; Audi's response to acceleration complaints, 136; confessing failings, 137–140; Deepwater Horizon crisis, 28–30, 31, 133; drawing on reservoir of good will in, 142–145; Sprint's response to, 42–47; surrounding Toyota recalls, 128–130, 133, 135–137, 148–149

Cuddy, Amy, 26

Customer loyalty: allegiance to underdogs, 121; Amazon's prices generating, 96–98; Coca-Cola's, 34–36, 37, 38; corporate intention and, 33–34; cost of maintaining, 46–47; cultivating trust, 67–69; demonstrating, 53–54; deservingness and, 81; developing, 54–57, 119–120; e-commerce's effect on, 88–90, 98, 99; effect of competence without warmth on, 45–46; exchange relationships and, 41–42; losing, 10; Lululemon's, 61–69; predisposition toward trust, 66–67; principle of worthy intentions in, 64–67; reward programs for, 47–54; service creating, 146–148; short-circuiting with Groupon promotions, 87–90; Sprint's efforts to maintain, 42–45; transferring to brand, 7–10; turnarounds ensuring, 116–117; warmth and competence factors in, 34–36, 40–42; Zane's Cycles policy for, 78–80; Zappos' team for, 94–96, 98. See also Loyalty tests

Customers: apologizing to, 125–126, 130; asking for forgiveness, 109, 137–140; developing mass-media messages for, 9–10; finding lifetime value of, 79; listening to, 58–59; losing faith in companies, 10; maintaining relationships with, 13–17, 21; perceiving "one-way" thinking, 72–73; "Pizza Turnaround" and honesty to, 105–110; purchasing from people they knew, 6–7; putting them first, 125–126, 131–133; random acts of kindness to, 57, 96; recognized by merchants, 51–52; reorienting corporate accountability to, 14–15, 43–44; satisfaction with e-commerce, 88–90, 98, 99; transferring loyalties to abstract brands, 7–10; welcoming, 75–77; Zappos' loyalty to, 95. See also Customer loyalty

D

Dansko, 167
Data mining, 154, 155
Day, Christine, 63–64, 68–69
Deepwater Horizon crisis, 28–30, 31, 133
Dekoy, Bob, 58, 59
Deservingness, 81

Dillow, Tate, 114–115
Domino's Pizza: acknowledging unacceptable product, 105–106, 115, 116, 145; actions taken by leaders of, 120; ensuring customer loyalty, 116–117, 152; "Pizza Turnaround" campaign, 105–110, 114–116, 145; role as underdog, 121
Doyle, Patrick, 105, 107, 108–109, 110, 111, 112, 115, 116, 117, 121, 145, 152
Drucker Institute, 163
Drucker, Peter, 160

E

e-commerce. See Internet
eBay, 120–121
Embracing change, 156–159
Employees: effect of Groupon promotions on, 86–87; leaders inspiring transformation among, 112–114; working for companies with worthy intentions, 168
Envy Up, Scorn Down (Fiske), 27
Etsy, 167
Euro RSCG, 111
Exchange relationships, 41–42
Exline, Julie Juola, 138
Expedia, 88–90

F

Facebook: downside of companies on, 103; maintaining relationships on, 100–101; Panera Bread account on, 20
Faddis, Dr. Kelly, 50, 54–57
Federal Reserve Bank of Kansas City, 48, 49

First impressions, 55
Fiske, Susan T., 3–4, 8, 25–26, 28–31, 133
Ford, 133
Ford v. Dodge, 163
Forgiveness: asking for, 109, 137–140; changes in motivation with, 145–146; human nature of, 5
Forrester Research, 44
Fortier, Suzanne, 19, 20, 21
Fournier, Susan, 28
Frequent-flyer miles, 47

G
Gap, 5
GE, 164
Generosity, 21
Giveaways, 79–80
Glick, Peter, 26
Goldman Sachs, 30, 31, 133, 137
Goldman, Seth, 16
Google, 154–155
Gorsky, Alex, 149
Green Apron Book (Starbucks), 75
Groupon, 85–90

H
Harper, David, 72
Hayward, Tony, 30, 107
Health care: creating shared value, 164; developing customer-based, 54–57; Tylenol recalls, 28, 29, 30, 31, 131–132, 142–144, 148, 149
Heinz, 6
Hershey, 32–34, 37, 38, 119–120
Hesse, Dan, 42, 46–47, 121, 152
Hoch, Stephen, 49–50
Honda, 133

Honest Tea: actions taken by leaders of, 120; aligning efforts with warmth and competence, 159; cultivating trust, 66; goal of honesty and transparency in, 16–17; underdog image of, 122
Hotels.com, 88–90
Hsieh, Tony, 121
Hulsey, Clare, 35

I
Identification with values, 116–117, 118
Intentions. *See* Worthy intentions
InterContinental Hotel, 53
Internalization of values, 117, 118
Internet: building relationships on, 90–91; e-commerce and customer loyalty, 88–90, 98, 99; gaging company's perceived presence on, 90–92; mass market advertising on, 102–103; perceptions of warmth on sites, 93; taking Loyalty Test on, 153; undermining earlier economic forces, 11
Ivory soap, 8–9

J
Jobs, Steve, 118
Johnson & Johnson: creating shared value, 164; Tylenol recalls, 28, 29, 30, 31, 131–132, 133, 142–144, 148, 149
Johnson, Bob, 44
Journal of Consumer Psychology, 31

K
Kaye, Peter, 17
Kervyn, Nico, 28, 31, 131, 133

Khan, Dr. Mehmood, 165
Koch, Jim, 110, 112
Kraft, 163
Kramer, Mark, 160, 164
Kumarasamy, Sundar, 72

L
Labus, Shaea, 95
Larson, Erik, 10
Leaders: asking for forgiveness, 109; becoming transformational, 113–114; Branson's role as underdog, 123–126; CEOs as spokespeople, 107–108, 110–111; dealing with unacceptable product, 105–106, 115, 116, 130, 145; establishing trust, 110–112, 120; expectation of values voiced by, 118–119; inspiring employees, 112–114; pursuing standards vs. maximizing profits, 163–164; role in marketing, 105–108
Levi Strauss, 6
Lifetime value of customers, 79–80
Liker, Jeffrey K., 149
Listening to customers: embracing feedback from customers, 156–159; examples of, 58–59; Lululemon's crisis and, 69, 74–75
L.L. Bean, 81
Loeber Motors, 58
Los Angeles Times, 128
Loyalty tests: passing, 59; rewarding programs and, 47–54; Sprint's efforts to pass, 42–45; website for, 153
Lululemon: aligning efforts with warmth and competence, 159; building Internet relationships,

90–91; building warmth factor at, 62–63; cultivating loyal customers, 65–66; customer support for, 61–62; effect of recall on customers, 68–69; listening to customers, 69, 74–75; profitability of, 63–64

M
Mackey, John, 107, 108
Macy's, 92–94
Mad Men, 9
Malone, Chris, 3–4, 27, 28–31, 70, 71, 72, 75, 92, 133, 146–148
Manet, Édouard, 6
Manning, Harley, 44
Marketing: Branson's use of Virgin name, 124–125; CEOs as spokespeople, 107–108, 110–111; dealing with shift to mass production, 6–7; deceptive public relations in, 120–121; evolution of, 10; honesty and transparency in, 17; Montgomery Ward's, 7–8; Relationship Renaissance within, 14–17; Tylenol repackaging campaign, 131–132
Marketing. See also Advertising; Brands; Reward programs; Stories
Marlboro, 30, 31
Martin, Ed, 34
Maslow, Abraham, 17
McDonald's, 29, 157–158
McNeil Consumer Healthcare unit, 28, 29, 34, 133, 142–143
Mercedes Benz, 30, 31, 57
Merchants: protecting reputations, 13; purchasing from those you

knew, 6–7; recognizing customers,
51–52. *See also* Companies
Method, 167
Michelangelo phenomenon,
156–157, 158
Milton Hershey School, 32
Minute Maid, 29
Montgomery Ward, 7–8
Moynihan, Brian, 107

N
Naked Consumer, The (Larson), 10
Nalebuff, Barry, 16
National Highway Transportation
and Safety Administration
(NHTSA), 128–129, 135
Nestlé, 164
Netflix, 5
New and Improved (Tedlow), 7–8
New York Times, 16, 43
New York Times Magazine, 154
Nextel, 42–43
NHTSA (National Highway
Transportation and Safety
Administration), 128–129,
135
Nonprofit organizations: loyalty in
annual giving to, 69–74; warmth
and competence in charitable
giving, 71–74
Nooyi, Indra, 118, 161, 163, 164
Nordstrom's, 40, 67

O
Online travel agencies (OTAs),
88–90
Orbitz, 88–90
Orvis, 81, 82
Out-groups, 26

P
Panera Bread, 19–21, 120
Papa John's Pizza, 110
Parkinson, Andrew, 147–148
Patagonia, 164, 165, 166
People: attraction to warmth, 24;
forgiving companies, 109, 137–140;
innate perceptions of warmth and
competence, 2–3, 22–23; judging
companies on their, 33; perceiving
human face as first brand, 24,
37; personal brand relationships
of, 28; predicting responses with
warmth and confidence theory,
25–27; predisposition toward trust,
66–67; prejudice inherent in, 27;
purchasing from merchants they
knew, 6–7; relating competence
and bodily stances, 24; working for
companies with worthy intentions,
168
Pepsi Refresh Project, 118
PepsiCo: community grants from,
118; company makeover at, 161–
163, 164; rebalancing priorities at,
165
Peters, Tom, 13
Philanthropic acts: community grants
from PepsiCo, 118; increasing brand
preference with, 119–120; Panera
Bread's, 20, 21; testing effect on
brands, 32–34
"Pizza Turnaround" campaign,
105–110, 114–116, 145
Plum Organics, 167
Porsche, 30, 31
Porter, Michael E., 160, 164, 167
Posies Bakery and Cafe, 86–87
Prejudice, 27

Prices: generating loyalty on Amazon, 96–98; in Groupon promotions, 86–90; relationship-based loyalty and higher, 81

Principle of worthy intentions. *See* Worthy intentions

Procter & Gamble, 3, 8–9

Products: acknowledging unacceptable, 105–106, 115, 116, 145; apologizing for failures in, 111, 125–126, 130, 140–142; refocusing, 162; tracking quality via social networks, 115–116

Profitability: customer loyalty linked with, 46–47; Lululemon's, 63–64; pursuing standards vs. maximizing, 163–164

Publix, 90

R

Random acts of kindness, 57, 96

Recalls: analyzing warmth and competence in, 132–133; finding moments of truth in, 12; Toyota safety, 128–130, 133, 135–137, 148–149; Tylenol, 28, 29, 30, 31, 131–132, 133, 142–144, 148, 149

Reinventing the Wheel (Zane), 78

Relationship Renaissance: Amazon's place in, 98; benefit corporations in, 165–166; business self-awareness in, 152–156; celebrity endorsements in, 111; cultivating loyalty in, 36, 37, 38, 65–66; embracing significant change, 156–159; establishing trust with leaders, 110–112; learning from mistakes in, 148–150; shifting priorities in, 159–168; social accountability in, 14–18; Ulukaya's success in, 83

Relationships: effect of e-commerce on, 88–90, 98, 99; exchange vs. communal, 41–42; feeling empathy in, 145–146. *See also* Relationship Renaissance

Reputation: developing deservingness, 81; protecting company's, 13–14. *See also* Worthy intentions

Reward programs: alternatives to, 65–66; corporate costs of, 48–49; designing limitations for, 50; e-commerce effects on, 88–90; frequent-flyer, 47; recognizing customers with, 51–52; repeat customers without, 96; rethinking, 49–50; shortcomings in, 50–53; slippage in, 50

Rolex, 30, 31

Rolls Royce, 30, 31

S

S&H Green Stamps, 51

Sales: Branson's background in, 123; satisfying customers for, 58–59

Sam Adams Beer, 110

Saylor, Mark, 127–128, 130, 135, 137

Schnatter, John, 110, 111–112

Sears, 92–94

Seventh Generation, 167

Shell, 28, 29

Simply Measured, 100–101

Slippage in reward programs, 50

Social accountability: reorienting business to customer, 14–15, 43–44; updated adages for era of,

15; Verizon's response to online protests, 15

Social media: promoting Chobani yogurt, 82; threat of YouTube advertising in, 107–108

Social networks: account of Panera Bread on, 20–21; advertising moving into, 102–103; building business via, 56; creating instant karma within, 14–15; developing relationships on, 100; role in customer relationships, 99–101; tracking product quality using, 115–116; understanding principle of trust in, 66–67

Social responsibility. *See* Worthy intentions

Solano, Brandon, 105, 109–110

Southwest, 5

Sperry & Hutchinson Company, 51

Sprint, 42–47, 121, 152

Starbucks, 75–77

Stereo content model (SCM), 26

Sthanunathan, Stan, 35

Stories: about companies as underdog, 119–122; CEOs as spokespeople in company, 107–108, 110–111; publicized on social networks, 21; Virgin's David vs. Goliath image in, 123–126

Subway, 88

Survivor, 1–2

T

Tabasco, 6

Target, 79, 154, 155

Tedlow, Richard, 7–8

Toyodo, Akio, 130

Toyota: emphasis on competence at, 133, 135–137; negative publicity around San Diego crash, 129–130; recall by, 128–130, 133, 135–137, 148–149

Toyota Under Fire (Liker), 149

Trader Joe's, 49

Transactional leadership, 113

Transformational leadership, 113–114

Transparency: Apple's lack of, 141–142; Domino's, 105–110, 145; handling Tylenol recalls, 143–144; as Honest Tea goal, 17; importance in crises, 138

Tropicana, 28

Trust: BP's loss of public, 29–30; conditional and unconditional, 67–68; cultivating, 67–69; judging trustworthiness, 23; predisposition toward, 66–67; Toyota's loss of, 128–130

Twitter, 100–101

Tylenol: loyalty of customers to, 38; recalls, 28, 29, 30, 31, 131–132, 133, 142–144, 148, 149; warmth and competence ratings for, 133

U

Ulukaya, Hamadi, 81–83

Underdog stories, 120–126

Unilever, 122, 164

University of Dayton, 69–74

U.S. Postal Service, 31

V

Verizon, 15, 146–148

Veteran's Administration, 31

Virgin Group, 123–126

W

Wal-Mart, 77, 79, 92–94, 164

Wall Street Journal, 132

Wallace, Ed, 65

Walton, Sam, 118

Warmth: assessing, 22; corporate qualities of, 39–42; evaluating in charitable giving, 71–74; fueling competence with, 75; Groupon crowding and perceived, 87; judging trustworthiness from, 23; overreliance on competence vs., 8; perceiving and judging person's, 2; providing reservoir of good will, 144–145; responding to websites with, 91–92; shown in welcoming customers, 75–77; Toyota's emphasis on competence vs., 133, 135–137. *See also* Warmth and competence theory

Warmth and competence theory: analyzing customer loyalty to Coca-Cola, 34–36, 37, 38; applying, 4–5, 27–34; authors' research in, 3–4; composite ratings for companies, 134; instant assessments of, 22–23; predicting behavioral responses with, 25–27; Tylenol recalls and, 142–144, 148, 149

Wartzman, Rick, 163

Weiner, Russell, 105–106, 114–115

Wellman, Barry, 15

Whitworth, Ralph, 162–163

Whole Foods, 107, 108

Wilson, Chip, 63

Winfrey, Oprah, 111, 118

Worthy intentions: about, 12; competitive edge using, 77–80; confessing failings, 137–140; cultivating trust, 67–69; defined, 64; developing reputation for deservingness, 81; finding employees who demonstrate, 148; overcoming "one-way" thinking, 72–73; quantifying social responsibility, 33–34; Starbuck's Five Ways of Being, 75–77; testing effect on purchases, 32–34; working for companies with, 168; Zappos' demonstration of, 95–96. *See also* Philanthropic acts; Social accountability; Trust

Z

Zane, Chris, 77–80

Zappos: aligning efforts with warmth and competence, 159; bought by Amazon, 98, 122; customer loyalty team at, 94–96, 98; turning to service-centered strategy, 121; warmth factor at, 92–94

Zeta Interactive, 107